'WE ARE STILL DIDENE'

Stories of Hunting and History from Northern British Columbia

Detailing the history of the Aboriginal village of Iskut, British Columbia, over the past one hundred years, 'We Are Still Didene' examines the community's transition from subsistence hunting to wage work in trapping, guiding, construction, and service jobs. Drawing from extended transcripts of stories told by the group's hunters, Thomas McIlwraith explores how Iskut hunting culture and the memories that the Iskut share have been maintained orally.

McIlwraith demonstrates the ways in which these stories challenge the idealized images of Aboriginals that underlie state-sponsored traditional ecological knowledge studies, as well as illustrating how the narratives are connected to the Iskut Village's complex relationships with resource extraction companies and the province of British Columbia, and to their interactions with animals and the environment.

(Anthropological Horizons)

THOMAS MCILWRAITH is an instructor in the Department of Sociology and Anthropology at Douglas College.

ANTHROPOLOGICAL HORIZONS

Editor: Michael Lambek, University of Toronto

This series, begun in 1991, focuses on theoretically informed ethno-graphic works addressing issues of mind and body, knowledge and power, equality and inequality, the individual and the collective. Interdisciplinary in its perspective, the series makes a unique contri-bution in several other academic disciplines: women's studies, history, philosophy, psychology, political science, and sociology.

For a list of the books published in this series see page 167.

THOMAS McILWRAITH

'We Are Still Didene'

Stories of Hunting and History from Northern British Columbia

UNIVERSITY OF TORONTO PRESS
Toronto Buffalo London

© University of Toronto Press 2012
Toronto Buffalo London
www.utppublishing.com
Printed in Canada

ISBN: 978-1-4426-4324-6 (cloth)
ISBN: 978-1-4426-1173-3 (paper)

Printed on acid-free and 100% post-consumer recycled paper with
vegetable-based inks.

Library and Archives Canada Cataloguing in Publication
McIlwraith, Thomas, 1969–
'We are still didene' : stories of hunting and history from northern
British Columbia / Thomas McIlwraith.

(Anthropological horizons)
Includes bibliographical references and index.
ISBN 978-1-4426-4324-6 (bound)   ISBN 978-1-4426-1173-3 (pbk.)

1. Tahltan Indians – Hunting – British Columbia – Iskut – History.
2. Tahltan Indians – British Columbia – Iskut – History.   3. Traditional
ecological knowledge – British Columbia – Iskut.   4. Oral history – British
Columbia – Iskut.   I. Title.   II. Series: Anthropological horizons

E99.T12M45 2012   971.1'8004972   C2012-902213-6

Chapter 3 was previously published in the journal *Anthropological
Linguistics* by University of Nebraska Press. It is reprinted here with
permission.

This book has been published with the help of a grant from the Canadian
Federation for the Humanities and Social Sciences, through the Awards to
Scholarly Publications Program, using funds provided by the Social
Sciences and Humanities Research Council of Canada.

University of Toronto Press acknowledges the financial assistance to its publishing program of the Canada Council for the Arts and the Ontario Arts Council.

 Canada Council   Conseil des Arts
for the Arts   du Canada

 ONTARIO ARTS COUNCIL
CONSEIL DES ARTS DE L'ONTARIO

University of Toronto Press acknowledges the financial support of the
Government of Canada through the Canada Book Fund for its publishing
activities.

For the Elders of Iskut Village

Proceeds from the publication of this book go to the Iskut Elders Fund

Contents

Illustrations

(Photos not otherwise credited were taken by the author.)

Acknowledgments

I am indebted to a large number of people who made my research possible and who offered me the intellectual support that I needed to write this book. The people of Iskut Village, in northwestern British Columbia, have been incredibly welcoming and kind to me throughout several years of visiting and working in their community. Always while writing, I have tried to be true to the people who shared their time and lives with me; in turn, I am trying to share something of myself with them through my writing. This book is evidence of my efforts to reveal myself – my interest and my ignorance – to Iskut people. All mistakes and misinterpretations are mine. I can only hope that they will allow me to continue learning about their culture.

First and foremost, I thank Arthur Nole, Louis Louie, and the late Robert Quock. Their stories and words are central to the book. I am grateful for their generous permission, or the permission of their descendants, to reproduce the stories they shared with me. They remain the rights holders of their stories. Likewise, I claim no ownership to any of the words or stories of other people included in this book.

My thanks go to the village elders who shared substantial time with me. These people include Ellen Dennis, Gertie Dennis, James Dennis, Mabel Dennis, the late Mathew Henyu, Agnes Hunter, Louis Louie, Morris Louie, Regina Louie, Rita Louie, the late Philip Louie, Arthur Nole, Loveman Nole, Sarah Nole, Jenny Quock, Peggy Quock, and the late Robert Quock. To all of you, *medūh*, thank you.

Many other people helped me, accepted me into their families, or took me under their wings at Iskut Village. I thank Chief Louis Louie and the members of the Iskut First Nation Council in 2002. They supported my work. Current Chief Marie Quock and her council have continued that support. Thanks also to members of the band staff, who 'tolerated' my bad coffee and my presence in their offices. Sally Havard helped facilitate my work and has been a good friend over several years. I also thank Iskut community members and other Tahltans: Theresa Abou, Erma Bourquin, Jim Bourquin, Camille Callison, Huey Carlick, the late Jackie Carlick, Judy Carlick, Amanda Dennis, Angela Dennis (who helped with the Tahltan-language transcriptions), Odelia Dennis, Wayne Dennis, Misty Jakesta-Louie, Alec Joseph, Andy Louie, Bertha Louie, Feddie Louie, Floyd Louie, Heather Louie, Paul Louie, Penny Louie, Sharon Marion, Vern Marion, Kathleen Morin, Father J.M. Mouchet, Annabel Nole, Connie Nole, Doyle Nole, Jim Nole, Maggie Nole, Ruby Nole, Jerry Quock, Marie Quock, Mary Quock, Ramona Quock, Curtis Rattray, and Pauline Wall. I thank the children, teenagers, and younger adults for teaching me about their homes and their passions for hunting, fishing, and travelling. In particular, I learned a lot from Alfie Day, Mike Day, Frances Marion, Kelsey Marion, Shelby Marion, and Dustin Nole. Wade Davis and Gail Percy talked with me about Iskut history and have always taken considerable interest in my research. Janice Sheppard offered insights into her Iskut fieldwork and shared her Athapaskan library with me. Thank you all.

This book has benefited from the stimulating intellectual environment I found at the University of New Mexico in Albuquerque. My doctoral committee chair and mentor, David W. Dinwoodie, has challenged my thinking and supported my intellectual and fieldwork interests for years. Keith H. Basso and Sylvia Rodriguez never stopped pushing me to think harder and to write better. Robert A. Brightman (Reed College) encouraged me to consider the connections between my data and broader scholarship on Aboriginal hunting and history. Graduate school would not have been nearly as fascinating, intellectually rewarding, or fun without my graduate student colleagues. Thanks particularly to Jill Ahlberg Yohe, Steve Gooding, Lars Kuelling, Philip Laverty, Mariann Skahan, Sarah Soliz, and Patrick Staib.

I was fortunate to receive funding for this research. I was the recipient of a graduate fellowship from the Social Sciences and Humanities Research Council of Canada. The Endangered Languages Fund gave me monies to document animal stories in the Tahltan language (2002–03). The Jacobs Fund of the Whatcom Museum in Bellingham, Washington also provided funds for me to document animal names and stories (2002–03). Likewise, several groups at the University of New Mexico, including the Department of Anthropology, the Office of Graduate Studies, and the Graduate and Professional Student Association provided monies for me to pursue my research objectives. Douglas College, my employer in New Westminster, British Columbia, generously provided funding for research and manuscript editing. I was also granted a leave from teaching in the fall of 2009 to complete this manuscript. The support of the Douglas College community has been invaluable and is much appreciated.

I presented early drafts of some of these chapters at academic meetings and in public lectures. I gave a paper on hunting stories at the meetings of the American Anthropological Association in Chicago in November 2003. It was later published in the journal *Anthropological Linguistics* (McIlwraith 2008), and it appears here as chapter 3 with permission from the publisher, University of Nebraska Press. I spoke about guiding stories at the meetings of the American Society for Ethnohistory in Chicago in November 2004 and at a lecture sponsored by the Maxwell Museum Association of the University of New Mexico; those addresses form the basis of chapter 5.

My professional colleagues have helped me with this work. Robert N. Diaz, my long-time friend and business and academic colleague, has shown unfailing interest in my work; without our talks during drives around British Columbia this book would be much the worse. Conversations about Tahltan linguistics with John Alderete (Simon Fraser University) have been invaluable; generously, John shared his own research with me. My colleagues at Douglas College have offered a collegial place to teach; talking about anthropology with Laurie Beckwith and Tim Paterson has been fruitful and enjoyable. I also thank Ellen Morgan, Robert J. Muckle (Capilano University), Bjorn Simonsen, and Marni Westerman (Douglas College). Conversations with Bruce G. Miller (University of British Columbia) and John Barker (University of British Columbia), mentors and friends, continue to enrich and influence my career. Thanks to Patrick Moore (University of British Columbia) for helpful suggestions throughout this process. I remember my students here too; they have asked difficult questions and taught me to explain my understanding of Aboriginal life in British Columbia more clearly. Regarding this manuscript, Keren Rice kindly assisted me with the notes on orthographic and transcription conventions. Two anonymous reviewers pushed me to make the wider relevance of the hunting stories more obvious. The manuscript is improved for the care shown by John Parry during an extensive and thorough edit. Jill McConkey at the University of Toronto Press provided thoughtful comments on the text.

My entire academic career owes significantly to my conversations with my father and mother, Thomas F. and Duane McIlwraith. I would not have come this far without their interest and continuing encouragement. And, finally, I thank my wife, Mariela, and my children, Thomas and Alessandra, for putting up with all of my travelling and time living away from home. That is a remarkable gift.

Notes on Orthographic and Transcription Conventions

The sounds of the Tahltan language, as spoken by the people at Iskut Village in 2002, are represented in this work in the practical orthography, following Carter, Carlick, and Carlick (1994). The pronunciation key given here (see tables 1 and 2) provides English-language equivalents for Tahltan sounds and is based on the key developed by Carter in *Basic Tahltan Conversation Lessons* (Carter 1991, iii–v). The letters are given in Tahltan alphabetical order.

There is some variation in pronunciation among Tahltan speakers. Leer (1985) proposes to use the symbol s̲ for a sound that varies between the th sound in the English word *thing* and the English s sound in the word *sing*. The symbol z̲ likewise represents th in an English word like *that* or the z sound in an English word like *zoo*. Thus, some people pronounce the word s̲a'e, 'long time ago,' as sa'e, and others pronounce it with as tha'e, where th represents the sound in *thing*. Similar variation is found with ts̲, ts̲', and dz̲. For further information on Tahltan phonology, see Hardwick (1984) and Nater (1989) for comprehensive introductions to the Tahltan sound system. Alderete (2005) provides a thorough review of tone and length. Bob (1999), a person with Tahltan ancestry and a Master's degree in linguistics, describes Tahltan laryngeal phenomena with particular attention to the bilabial stop b. See also an annotated bibliography of Tahltan-language resources, written by Alderete and McIlwraith (2008).

In most transcripts, I follow the style of Robert E. Moore (1993), who sets transcripts into columns. Text lined up to the left represents the narrative frame whereby the storyteller talks directly to the audience. Speech in the second column from the left represents third-person

Table 1 Consonants

Tahltan Practical Orthography	English Equivalent	Phonetic Description*
'(glottal stop)	a stoppage of air in the throat like the stoppage in the middle of the English phrase uh_oh	ʔ
b	b in *big*	b
ch	ch in *church*	tš
ch'	same as ch but with a stoppage in throat	tš'
d	d in *dad*	d
dl	no English equivalent; often sounds like gl in *glue*	dl
dz	ds in *pads*	dz
dz̲	Similar to *add the* in English if said quickly.	dð
g	g in *good*	g
gh	g in back of throat; soft g	ɣ
h	h in *head*	h
j	j in *joke*	dž
k	k in *king*	k
k'	same as k but with a stoppage in throat	k'
kh	softer k, said in the back of the throat. Similar to some English pronunciations of the name of the composer *Bach* or Spanish pronunciations of the j in *jalapeño*.	x
l	l in *large*	L
ł	no English equivalent; for some, it sounds like the l in kl sequences like *Klondike*	ł
m	m in *mother*	M
n	n in *no*	N
nh	no English equivalent; like an n with a puff of air after it	ṇ
p	p in *pup* (rarely heard in Tahltan)	P
s	s in *see*	S
s̲	th in *thin*; this is pronounced like s in *see* by some speakers (see below)	θ
sh	sh in *shoot*	Š
t	t in *ten*	t
t'	t with stoppage in throat	t'
tl	no English equivalent; often sounds like kl in *Klondike*	tł

Table 1 (*continued*)

Tahltan Practical Orthography	English Equivalent	Phonetic Description*
tl'	tl with stoppage in throat	tɬ'
ts	ts in the name *Patsy*	ts
ts'	ts with stoppage in throat	ts'
t<u>s</u>	no English equivalent; similar to t followed by th in *thin*	tθ
t<u>s</u>'	t<u>s</u> with stoppage in throat	tθ'
w	w in *water*	w
y	y in *yes*	y
z	z in *zoo*	z
<u>z</u>	th in *then*; pronounced like z in *zoo* by some speakers (see below)	ð

* The phonetic descriptions of both consonants and vowels are those associated with 'Athapaskan IPA,' a system which is more common in Athapaskan linguistics than IPA. The use of the Athapaskan IPA system avoids confusions that stem from comparisons between IPA and the Tahltan Practical Orthography. These confusions include the observation that, in Tahltan, voiced stops d and g are actually the unvoiced stops t and p respectively (John Alderete, personal communication, 27 July 2010).

Table 2 Vowels

Tahltan Practical Orthography	English Equivalent	Phonetic Description
a	usually like the u in *cup*	a
e	e in ten	e
i	i in *bit*; sometimes ee in *keep*	i
o	o in *oats*	o
u	oo in *boot*	u
ā	like au in *caught*	a:
ē	same as e but longer	e:
ī	like i but longer	i:
ō	same as o but longer	o:
ū	same as u but longer	u:

narration of the actions of characters or participants in the stories. And the third column from the left quotes speech of story participants (Moore 1993, 219–20). Occasionally, I add editorial comments in square brackets offset from the rest of the text.

A final note: for readers who are unfamiliar with reading transcripts, I encourage you to start reading at the beginning of a transcript and simply read through the text as if the formatting was not there. In most cases, the stories are easily read and understood without any special knowledge of transcription protocols.

'WE ARE STILL DIDENE'

Stories of Hunting and History from
Northern British Columbia

Introduction: The Persistence of Hunting

In October 2002, at Iskut Village, British Columbia, my opportunities to record stories with village elders increased as people started spending more time at home. The first snows had fallen. The lakes were starting to freeze. Roadways were becoming icy. Travel throughout the area was becoming more difficult. Most Iskut families had settled into the routines of the school year. Employees of the Iskut First Nation were back at work after summer holidays. Almost everyone had abandoned lengthy camping trips to Stikine River fishing spots or to *Tl'abāne* hunting areas.[1] The yellow leaves of *k'is* ('mountain alder,' *Alnus incana*), so dramatic on hillsides in September, blanketed the ground. Winter was approaching, and people's thoughts were turning to cold-weather activities such as hunting *kedā* ('moose,' *Alces alces*) along the road, ice fishing, sewing, snowmobiling, and watching hockey on television.

One afternoon, I asked Arthur Nole[2] to tell animal stories to seven- and eight-year-olds at the Iskut school. Arthur is an Iskut elder in his early sixties. With my request to him, I hoped to satisfy the terms of a grant-funded project to compile a book and an audio disc of stories in Tahltan, the local language.[3] The idea for the book came from Julie Ross, the Iskut First Nation's education councillor, who hoped that students would use it in the classroom. I was, however, having a hard time finding people who were willing to talk with me in Tahltan and on tape. They told me they had more pressing things to do.

After some discussion about the purpose of the book, Arthur agreed to speak with the students. He also consented to my recording him on audio and video cassettes. The classroom teacher, a non-Iskut woman, was happy to have a new activity for her students. Catherine James, the school's Tahltan-language instructor, hoped that the session might

yield some useful material for generating teaching aids. It relieved me
to know that I was completing the terms of the grant.

Later in October, in a classroom surrounded by walls covered in
children's art projects, Arthur began talking from a chair at the front
of a classroom. He told a couple of stories about killing moose and
reminded the children about hunting safety. The youngsters listened
quietly, but on occasion interrupted him with their own hunting stories. When I asked Arthur to speak in Tahltan, he told the class about a
hunting trip. The account of that hunt is below.

Transcript 0.1: Moose Hunting Today and in the Past

[Setting: Arthur talks to five children; two teachers and one anthropologist are present. Arthur wears a microphone clipped on his shirt. A tape
recorder is on a table nearby. A video camera captures the event from
the back of the room.]

1   I say [said] it in English about hunting.

2   Now I say it in our language.   [Arthur repeats a story he has just
                                        told.]

3   Sa'e   [Conventional story introduction.]
    Long time ago

4   dāda ejinasīdel   kedā   kah
    when they all hunt   *moose*   *for*

5   desideł.
    they travel

6   Itāde   nisādi   hōnezesikhīn.
    Sometimes   *far away* *before they kill it.*

7   Sometimes maybe three hours' walk to where they izesikhīn.
    Sometimes maybe three hours walk to where they kill it.

8   They call,

9   they say,

10   āk'īdi
        kill site

11   where they kill moose.

12   That's what they call it in our language.

13   Kedā   izesikhīn   ekuchechāh.
        Moose   *they kill it*   *next day*

14   Then,   den   mekahdedel.
     Then,   *people*   *go get it.*

15   Tlī'gwele,
        Dog pack,

16   engwele.
        your pack.

17   That's how they bring moose.

18   Sa'e
        Long time ago

19   za'ahute,   za'ahute
        no good,   *no good.*

20   den   hoghanādił.
        people   *place where they go (to hunt)*

21   Today we use vehicles, but we still didene.[4]
     Today we use vehicles, but we are still Native people.

                                                    (9 October 2002)

Free Translation

Long time ago when our ancestors travel, they hunted for moose.
Sometimes they went far away before they kill one. Sometimes maybe
three hours' walk to where they killed it. They call, they say, kill site
where they kill moose. That's what they call it in our language.

The next day they kill a moose. Then they go get it. They pack with dogs and by themselves. That's how they bring moose.

Long time ago it was harder, where people went to hunt. Today we use vehicles, but we are still Native people.

Analysis

Arthur's story, I came to realize, is a stylized account of any hunt. It may in fact be a composite account of a number of previous hunting events. It is the kind of story – short, dense, and unelaborated – that I heard repeatedly when I was around hunters of all ages. The final utterance in the story is what most interests me. In a nostalgic, yet purposeful statement, Arthur concludes his narrative: *'Sa'e / za'ahute, za'ahute / den hoghanādił. /* Today we use vehicles, but we still *didene'* (lines 18–21).[5] It is here, with the shift from a third-person pronoun to the first person, that the story and its message become personal. Arthur speaks about changes to hunting practices while affirming a Native heritage. By doing so, he challenges non-Iskut people – trophy hunters, government bureaucrats, and non-Natives in the nearby towns of *Tatl'ah* and Terrace – whom Natives have heard asking how one can reconcile the use of tools such as trucks and rifles with a tradition of hunting for food. Arthur's words establish a connection between past hunting practices, such as walking, and the use of current technologies, such as vehicles. And his comments contain an underlying political sentiment: adaptation to and acceptance of cultural change are reasonable and clever (also Nadasdy 2005, 315). For these reasons, Arthur's words – 'we are still *didene'* – form the title of this book.

Arthur's story exemplifies overlapping orientations in the lives of Iskut Villagers and lays out the theme of debating the present with evidence of the past that is central to this book. In talk, story, and action, Iskut people debate about the apparent opposition of participating in a sustenance hunting culture and working for a wage – and what those activities mean for remaining *didene*.[6] On the one hand, they speak with enthusiasm and pride about hunting and food animals and continue to hunt with interest and intensity. On the other hand, almost all of them work in the Canadian wage-based and industrial economy, and they value wage work highly for the material rewards it makes possible, such as trips to Las Vegas and mail-order purchases. They

Hunters look for animals with telescope in the *Tl'abāne*, August 2009.

easily reconcile hunting with the wage work that, in most cases, allows them to continue hunting.

It is outsiders, non-Natives typically, who sometimes assert that Iskut people should not operate in the two worlds of sustenance hunting and capitalism. Modernization and acculturation are one-way processes, they claim: industrialism leads to economic salvation, and it is better to leave hunting in the past because it only perpetuates poverty (Jarvenpa 1998). Renowned big-game outfitter Tommy Walker says as much in his memoirs: he employed many Iskut men and women as guides and cooks during the 1950s and 1960s and writes about their families' poverty (Walker 1976, various dates). Many Iskut people have read his book and reject his observations about their lives. Indeed, Arthur may have had Walker and his book in mind when he spoke, for his words refute Walker's characterizations of Iskut people. Arthur sees the use of vehicles in a hunt as consistent with being *didene*, a Native person; hunting is a current and worthwhile activity.

The interest of outsiders in Iskut hunting lands and resources began during the fur trade and guiding eras. In those days, Iskut people frequently participated in those economic ventures. In the last few years, outsiders have turned their gaze towards the hunting territories again, and Iskut people are questioning their interests and resisting their activities. Mineral wealth in the form of coal and coal-bed methane gas lies beneath the *Tl'abāne*. Resource companies such as Fortune Minerals and Shell Canada own rights to extract those minerals. Some Iskut people are curious to know the extent of the resources, which may offer them opportunities in mineral extraction. Others have protested vigorously against any effort to find out what is there. Blockades by Iskut people and the arrests of their elders demonstrate the intensity of their resistance. Uncertainty about the best way to proceed underscores historical and family divisions in the community.

The range of reactions to recent resource exploration in the *Tl'abāne* reflects the tension between tradition and change – between hunting and making money – that has existed in Iskut for generations. But, to listen to Arthur Nole, and to other community members who speak through this book, one would conclude that they think both positions are worthy of discussion. And, more important, they indicate that both positions are consistent with being proudly *didene*.

PART I

Background

1 Aboriginal Hunting in an Era of Traditional Ecological Knowledge

Introduction

For several generations, Iskut Villagers have reacted with stories and actions to suggestions by outsiders that their hunting economy reflects poverty and an inability to survive in the bush of northwestern British Columbia. They insist instead that they have always managed well, despite any hardship. They also say that they have always confidently challenged outsiders who arrive to exploit local animal populations, and more recently minerals, for financial gain. Since 1962, they have lived on a reserve, and questions about their knowledge about local lands persist. Cultural researchers and government bureaucrats inquire about traditional ecological knowledge (TEK) whenever proposals surface for the development or extraction of resources. TEK has become one marker of Iskut knowledge about local lands, and the ability of bureaucrats to identify, document, and distribute TEK marks their consultations with the community. Increasingly, Iskut people themselves harness TEK when they seek to influence outsiders' decisions about their traditional lands.

Despite its prevalence in some government studies, Iskut knowledge about food and animals resists easy interpretation or standard forms of analysis. Any attempt to isolate TEK from Iskut talk is highly problematic because hunting knowledge is found in most Iskut activities. Moreover, it is difficult to understand the importance of hunting in the lives of Iskut people because it is rarely discussed explicitly. Instead, expressions of hunting knowledge frequently appear artistically in the form of narratives. Sharing hunting memories, reporting animal kills, describing the follies of selfish hunters, or talking about uses of traditional lands includes the deft application of ellipsis, allusion, indirection, metaphor, and allegory. By analysing Iskut Villagers' use of these rhetorical devices and by identifying their complex relationships with animals and the environment, we can grasp that their talk of the hunt challenges the images of idealized, perhaps romantic, Aboriginal relations with the environment that underlie many TEK studies.

It seems obvious that named Aboriginal groups such as 'the Iskut people' would have a shared culture. Many non-Natives perceive individual BC Aboriginal groups as homogeneous entities with common history, territory, and language; the easy, taken-for-granted logic of a community name such as Iskut implies this. Yet the histories of Iskut's families are diverse. Iskut leaders and the Canadian government established the village only in the early 1960s (although many residents date permanent settlement back to at least the 1920s, and archaeological sites in the area indicate a long history of using the area). Today families hunt and camp in different places, pronounce Tahltan words differently, and use different labels for some fish species. All of this reflects disparate family origins in northern British Columbia. Iskut people face political demands for a unified history when the reality is somewhat different.

Hunting is the central metaphor that informs Iskut culture; understanding its role in the village is critical for understanding life there (Davis 2001, 27).[1] Further, I assert that hunting provides Iskut people with symbols that reflect cultural unity in a place where that is not always apparent (cf. Geertz 1973, 14, 17). Talk about the hunt deploys hunting symbols that include the animals themselves. Seemingly arcane sources of information, such as jokes, gossip, hunting memories, and personal histories, are rich in these symbols. These symbols provide hunters and everyone else with reference points for negotiating the impact of history and acting in a world where relations in the village and outside it are constantly changing. They help refute outsiders' perceptions that Iskut Natives are poor economically and culturally. And at times they help unite a community in which members have different places of origin and histories and that does not always see itself as homogeneous.

Iskut is an ethnic group in some ways. For Anthony D. Smith, 'an "ethnic group" is a type of community with a specific sense of solidarity and honor, and a set of shared symbols and values' (1981, 65). For him, members share ideas about common origins, history, and destiny and feel solidarity because of these common links (66). His observations reflect what bureaucrats and Iskut people themselves believe is central to claiming land in treaties or resource negotiations. To have a legitimate claim, a Native group must demonstrate something like ethnic identity – a common history – to the government, courts, and resource-extraction companies.

But I observed ambivalence at Iskut Village towards any idea of a unified ethnic identity. Iskut culture does not always map directly onto an ethnic identity in the terms that Smith lays out. The community sometimes looks like an ethnic group and at other times does not. Yet I do not necessarily believe that the group ceases to exist at times when ethnic unity is unclear. Iskut hunting talk creates solidarity, particularly in a place where common historical origins are difficult to identify.

Iskut hunting talk can thus form the basis for both government-sponsored ecological research *and* my anthropological interest in documenting Iskut's hunting culture ethnographically and in its contemporary expressions.[2] The results of my studies are these: hunting is a constant feature in the lives and culture of villagers; these people debate local history, and their values emerge through hunting activities and talk; and hunting unites families who lack common origins. Hunting remains central despite the encroachments and ambitions of outsiders. Its pervasiveness is not always readily apparent to outsiders, however, especially if they read history and ethnicity superficially. Group definitions at Iskut do not, it turns out, depend on everyone being the same as everyone else.

Motivation for the Study

The Iskut people have close cultural and political associations with Tahltan speakers in nearby *Tlēgōhīn* and *Tatl'ah*. I first met people from Iskut in the autumn of 1997 when Tahltan-speaking researchers from all three communities travelled to Victoria to learn how to use the provincial archives for studying Tahltan history. I helped with some of the research, and that led to my participation as a paid researcher and consultant in a Traditional Use Study (TUS) in 1998 and 1999.[3] The Tahltan political leadership in *Tatl'ah* and the BC Ministry of Forests jointly administered the TUS, which formed part of a province-wide program to fund Aboriginal organizations seeking to identify contemporary and historical land uses (Dinwoodie 2002, 2–5). Three Tahltan researchers formed the research team. Along with an historian colleague from Victoria and myself, the research team conducted archival research and interviews in an effort to document where Tahltan-speaking people hunted, fished, and collected plants. We also recorded place names and stories. Towards the end of the project, in May and June 1999, we travelled throughout the Tahltan traditional territory by truck, boat, helicopter, and floatplane photographing the places that we had identified. In the end, we produced a report, maps depicting about 1,400 places, and a computer database containing details of each one (Tahltan Joint Councils 1999).

The TUS program emerged from two major events in relations between the province and Native people. First, in 1991, British Columbia agreed to join the federal government and settle treaties with Aboriginal peoples. This move followed pressure from court decisions and the public, as well as from businesses seeking certainty over land and resource rights (McKee 2000, 30). For more than a century, the province had refused to negotiate treaties because, it maintained, Confederation in 1871 had extinguished Aboriginal title, if it had not evaporated earlier. Most BC Native groups, including the Iskut, do not have treaties with settler governments. The province's change of heart was a significant moment, and it spurred dozens of First Nations to issue statements of intention to negotiate a treaty. General research into historical land uses followed, and Traditional Use Studies became part of that effort.

Second, in 1997, the Supreme Court of Canada rendered its decision in a case about Aboriginal rights and land title – *Delgamuukw v. The Queen* (1997) – which admonished lower courts in British Columbia for not considering oral history as legitimate evidence in judgments about Aboriginal land and resource rights. In the 'Reasons for Judgment,' we read: 'The oral histories were used [in the original trial] in an attempt to establish occupation and use of the disputed territory which is an essential requirement for Aboriginal title. The trial judge refused to admit or gave no independent weight to these oral histories and then concluded that the appellants had not demonstrated the requisite degree of occupation for "ownership." Had the oral histories been correctly assessed, the conclusions on these issues of fact might have been very different.' (*Delgamuukw v. The Queen* 1997; cf. *Delgamuukw v. The Queen* 1991, 49). The decision sparked interest in Aboriginal research as Native groups sought to establish the legitimacy of their claims using oral traditions. And, the decision confirmed that BC Native people never ceded land to colonial or provincial officials (*Delgamuukw v. The Queen* 1997; also Culhane 1998).

Understanding the relationship between the BC treaty process, the *Delgamuukw* decision, and a study of hunting at Iskut Village requires an introduction to the patronizing attitudes and racist beliefs[4] about Native people by governments and non-Native people.[5] This racism towards Native people draws on ideas that Aboriginal foraging economies reflect impoverishment (Brody 2000; Jarvenpa 1998; Colpitts 2002, 41; Asch 1982, 348),[6] perceptions that Native people are intellectually inferior (Culhane 1998), ideas that the simplicity of Native cultures impedes social progress and development (Tennant 1990; Carlson 1997), and the notion that Natives are lazy (Lutz 2008, 31). Moreover, historians and anthropologists have documented systematic efforts by various federal and BC governments to marginalize and assimilate Native peoples and cultures and make 'Indians' more like 'whites' (Duff 1965; Coates 1991, 159–60; Lutz 2008). The best example is the Indian Act, which has, in its various amendments dating back to the 1870s, banned Native dances and ceremonies such as the potlatch and made it illegal for Native people to pursue land claims (Fisher 1977, 206–8; Tennant 1990, 45; Carlson 1997, 99). Parliament removed many of these provisions from the Indian Act in 1951, but the law's paternalism remains visible even today.

Recent examples of racism towards Native people appear in the context of Aboriginal land claims. A number of scholars cite the ruling of Justice McEachern in the original *Delagmuukw* decision (*Delgamuukw v. The Queen* 1991) as an example of the inability or unwillingness of British Columbians to see the complexity of Native cultures. In this regard, Furniss writes: '[McEachern] legitimated [his dismissal of the claims to Aboriginal ownership of land] by making several rather blunt assertions: that the early [Native people] were "primitive" people whose cultures were inherently inferior to those of civilized European society [and] that colonization had been in Aboriginal people's best interest' (Furniss 1999, 202; Miller 1992).

Furniss notes – and this is my point too – that McEachern ruled on the basis of a conventional and widespread view of noble yet primitive Natives (1999, 203). Furthermore, Furniss (1999, 13) and Tennant (1990, 15) both observe a paradox in the denial of Native land claims. On the one hand, some observers would deny Native people land and legal rights because they never had organized societies (e.g., *Delgamuukw v. The Queen* 1991); on the other hand, Native claims are invalid because their earlier social organization disappeared long ago through governmental assimilation and progress. Thus Aboriginal rights to lands and resources fall victim to contradictory ideas: that Native people are too different from (read: inferior) or too similar to (read: assimilated) non-Native people (Tennant 1990, 15).

Negative attitudes towards and perceptions of BC Native people spread beyond government policy. Furniss's monograph, *The Burden of History* (1999), is a detailed account of the relations between Secwepemc (formerly Shuswap; Interior Salish-speaking peoples) Native people and non-Natives in Williams Lake. Furniss is an anthropologist and land-claims researcher. She describes Williams Lake as a small, rural town, where a 'frontier cultural complex' – a penchant for whites to use assimilative thoughts, actions, and words to control public definitions of history – defines non-Native racism towards local Native people (20–21). Furniss details racism in the forms of private jokes about Indians, rituals relating to the Williams Lake Stampede, and public debates around land claims. She concludes that racist beliefs fester beneath a discourse of equality that assumes that assimilation is the only way whereby Native people, who are culturally inferior because of history or genetics, can advance and become like everyone else (191).

Furniss's experiences ring true for me. I have experienced awkward dinner conversations with non-Native friends about lazy Indians, egregious Native-rights claims, and excessive treaty settlements (also Furniss 1999, ix; Menzies 1994, 776; Foster 1998, 29–31). I have heard callers to radio talk shows in Vancouver complaining about Native people receiving too many handouts (see Ridington 1990a for a specific example). Newer forms of electronic media, such as readers' comments in on-line editions of newspapers, frequently contain these sentiments. And in 2006, in *Tatl'ah*, a row occurred on the Internet after a naïve newcomer to the area posted her 'observations' about Tahltan people on a blog. Apparently believing the blog was private, she described Tahltan people as incestuous, sexually promiscuous, and addicted to drugs. Months later, she posted an apology on the blog and then removed the blog from the Internet (original post: Anonymous, 5 September 2006; apology: Anonymous, 30 December 2006).

The racism that Furniss describes, McEachern invokes, and I overhear is apparent to Iskut people; they and their compatriots have encountered it for more than a century. Big-game guiding, of the kind that Tahltans participated in with outfitters like Tommy Walker, provides one example of racist assumptions in action. Historian Tina Loo notes that the idea of hunting for trophies derives from middle-class desires for anti-modern experiences (Loo 2001a). The primitiveness that they see in Native guides helps to satisfy such wishes: 'Though sports hunters viewed aboriginal guides with some mixture of admiration and disdain, their attitudes stemmed from prevailing racial ideas. Being "closer to nature," native peoples ... had an almost mystical understanding of the ways of the birds and the beasts, knowledge that made them desirable guides. But being closer to nature also meant aboriginals were inferior to whites. When a big game hunter hired an "Indian outfit," these contradictions were brought to the fore: in the field, the hunter and guide were both inferior and superior at the same time' (Loo 2001b, 312). Still, Loo indicates that Tahltan guides had strategies, akin to the pranks that appear in trickster mythology, to deal with the bravado, egotism, and implicit racism of the client hunters. From speaking Tahltan so that the clients could not understand their talk to walking quickly on trails or resting for far too long, they controlled their clients in the bush. That they faced, and learned to deal with, the imposition of inferiority on the basis of class and race was their experience of colonialism (Loo 2001b, 316).

In the stories in this book, the tradition of Iskut Tahltans sparring with outsiders continues. Stories such as Robert's account of wrangling horses (chapter 4) and political speeches such as Chief Louie's at *Hok'ats Łuwe Menh* (chapter 5) remind listeners and readers of the central role that Tahltan guides have played in the big-game hunting economy. They address struggles, literal and metaphorical, between Native guides themselves and between them and their non-Native clients. By extension, they demonstrate that Iskut people have for generations confronted colonialism and its expectations of them. With the recent arrival of oil and gas explorers from Shell Canada and Fortune Minerals, the outsiders simply have different names. They still appear with money and influence. They are supported by neo-liberal government policies, at both provincial and federal levels, that bolster a resource-extraction economy (Morgan 2009; Feit 2010, 55). But these outsiders have little understanding of why Iskut people fight to hunt and camp in the *Tl'abāne* or on Spatsizi Plateau.

The Tahltan Traditional Use Study, which concluded successfully under the terms of the contract with the province, left me with questions about the information that we had recorded and what it meant to the government, to Tahltan politicians, and to the villagers who participated in the research interviews. While the maps were impressive and the database was valuable because of the volume of information it contained, the most interesting data emerged from the stories of life at the places that we plotted on the maps. Typically, these stories remained on tape because we did not have the time to make verbatim transcriptions, and we were able to identify the locations of those places without doing so. The dissociation of geographical information from the experiences of those who told us about it made the work seem to me inadequate and incomplete (also Cruikshank 1998a, 52–53).

Since 2006, Tahltan people have been conducting much of the historical research themselves. They insist on what they call 'holistic presentations' of Tahltan culture in order to rectify the omissions and shortcomings of past projects, including the Traditional Use Study. For Tahltans, that study's inclusion of uncontextualized maps was unfortunate and unacceptable. Today, at minimum, any report for government must include statements by elders.

Documenting Traditional Ecological Knowledge

Like the Tahltan, I feel dissatisfaction with the representation of Native cultures and their food-gathering activities in government-sponsored research projects such as Traditional Use Studies. Typically, TUSs highlight locations or techniques of foraging activities and ignore the meanings these places hold for the people who know about them. They emphasize 'dots on maps' and use standard government topographic maps to create a context for the locations of culturally significant places. These administrative tools have little space to describe the social values of food gathering or explain various families' different hunting techniques. They offer even less detail about how hunters structure their hunting discussions.

My participation in such projects led me to search for other ways to record the rich experiences of Native people who continue to spend much time on the land. Traditional-use research left me curious about, for example, Native experts on local lands, animals, and fish who supplement sustenance practices with seemingly incongruous (and hard-to-map) work in office jobs, highway construction, or education. I speculated that a focus on the verbal aspects of hunting might reveal the activity's importance and meaning.

To answer the ethnographic and ecological questions that come to me from observing contemporary hunters, fishers, and gatherers, I turned first to ethnoecology.[7] Much of my field research consisted of my working with Iskut food collectors to document plant and animal names and harvesting techniques. In doing so, I engaged a long tradition in anthropology of ethnoscientific inquiry, or the study of linguistically labelled categories that people use when they talk about the world around them (e.g., Conklin 1954; Berlin 1966; Frake 1980 [1962]; Ellen 1986; Hunn 1990).

In a volume of collected essays on ethnoecology, Nazarea elaborates and indicates a recent shift in the research orientation of ethnoecologists. She suggests that studies of cognitive universals are giving way to concerns for 'how culture shapes cognition and mediates behavior' (Nazarea 1999, 6). She argues that earlier ethnoecologists missed an opportunity to link theoretical and applied environmental studies. Any refocusing of ethnoecology, she argues, must include paying greater attention to political and economic contexts. Because of the interest that some Iskut people have in using traditional ecological knowledge (TEK) and traditional use mapping – applied forms of ethnoecology – to respond to mining activities today, I agree. Like ethnoscience, TEK research documents the knowledge of Native people in local categories. It stresses the knowledge that people hold and share about elements of the natural environment, including animals, fish, and plants (Berkes 1999, 6–8).[8]

The documentation of TEK and efforts to use it bureaucratically evoke substantial criticism (Menzies and Butler 2006, 10–14), most emphatically from Cruikshank (1998b, 2005) and Nadasdy (1999, 2003).[9] Cruikshank worries about the reification of TEK as an object of scientific inquiry. She notes that few Western scholars see it as a system of understanding the world in and of itself. Rather, most study it when they want additional support for biological science (Cruikshank 1998b, 49). She observes that outsiders set the categories of TEK – Linnaean biological categories, for example. When researchers attempt to draw TEK from the frameworks in which it is known and used by local people and place it into the framework of science, they represent traditional knowledge as simple to their audiences. Its complexity is missed or ignored in the interest of, frequently, producing a report quickly.

Cruikshank extends her critique in *Do Glaciers Listen?* (2005), where she agrees that TEK is not inherently insidious. Her definition of 'local knowledge,' in fact, supports my challenge to the utility of TEK. Local knowledge is, she writes, 'tacit knowledge embodied in life experiences and reproduced in everyday behaviour and speech' (9).[10] However, she notes, government reports and scholars often portray local knowledge and TEK as static and timeless (10). Like Cruikshank, I have concerns about the reproduction and sharing of local knowledge between Iskut

Villagers and outsiders such as anthropologists and government representatives. These 'experts' ignore the life experiences that ground TEK, indeed even the ways in which it is learned and shared – as Arthur Nole shared it verbally with school children (introduction to this book). While it is possible to sift stories to isolate TEK, to mine a corpus of texts for facts about the environment, Iskut knowledge of animals has far deeper roots in everyday life than some TEK studies suggest. For this reason, my focus is largely on Iskut people using TEK rather than on deconstructing the concept itself.

Nadasdy examines how research and reports that use TEK reinforce power imbalances between Native communities and government agencies (Nadasdy 2003, 10). While most critics of TEK work note correctly that science and traditional knowledge do not mesh easily, bureaucrats pay only lip service to TEK. They offer money for TEK studies as a way of placating Native people who insist on its inclusion in consultations about resource development (117–18).[11] Most scientists and resource managers 'feel that ... drastic changes in the lifestyle of Aboriginal peoples have so eroded [TEK] that, effectively, it no longer exists' (118). Scientists engage in TEK research only to prevent protest against or interruption of their work.

Nadasdy's contention is provocative. It suggests that many bureaucrats feel that Native people do not have identifiable traditions today and possibly never did. This is part and parcel of the long-standing observation within anthropology that non-Natives seeking mythologies for Western civilization create the identities and images of Native people (e.g., Berkhofer 1978; Francis 1992 offers a Canadian perspective). In Berkhofer's terms, TEK is a characteristic of the 'white man's Indian.' By extension, TEK derives from romantic ideas about Natives who once lived as part of nature. But TEK emerges also from ideas of lost nobility, forgotten tradition, and the ability to express one's history in a non-Native medium. Paradoxically, TEK research assumes that Native people are knowledgeable, but not, in Arthur Nole's words, *didene* 'Native people' (transcript 0.1, line 21).

I have come to learn that hunting knowledge stored in a Traditional Use Study database means little to Iskut hunters. TUSs and TEK are tools of resource administrators, both in and out of Native communities, who usually decide which elements of TEK to use (Nadasdy 2007, 37). Researchers documenting TEK have recorded a great deal of information about foraging peoples, and, as Nadasdy hints, Native people have reasons for wanting it in reports: it gives some of them a voice in negotiations. It is one element of an Aboriginal voice in settings where outsiders demand validation of Aboriginal rights. Some Iskut hunters are also Iskut administrators and operate effectively in both worlds.

Ethnography

The Ethnography of Speaking about Hunting

The 'ethnography of speaking' helps me to overcome the limitations of TUSs and TEK research that governments and industrial developers sponsor. The ethnography of speaking, or of communication, is a perspective on the relationship between language and culture that highlights the context of speech production. As a framework for inquiry, it assists me in identifying the meanings that Iskut people associate with hunting, particularly when they do not speak freely or directly about them. It demands use of Iskut accounts of local history to explain why Iskut relationships with the land and its animals have remained constant in some cases and changed in others. It helps me understand why government and scientific circles continue to accept local knowledge, albeit in simplified or abbreviated form; the inclusion of TEK, they hope, will satisfy requirements to consult with First Nations.[12]

Iskut hunters present their stories of hunting and history with creativity and variation. With the ethnography of speaking as a theoretical and methodological guide, we can identify some general characteristics of hunting and historical narratives; examples appear in chapters 3 and 4. The stories are usually short, lasting from thirty seconds up to two minutes. They derive from the speaker's experiences and are not usually accounts of the experiences of others. Different Iskut hunters tend to organize hunting narratives in similar ways. This common structure suggests that people have talked about these events with each other previously. We might therefore conclude that the events are less relevant or important than simply engaging others in direct talk about hunting or history. Yet they include references to the common experiences all Iskut hunters share. They frequently expand into broader discussions of individual experiences. Hunting talk of this sort also includes points of reference for commenting on and managing social relationships within families and across family lines. By establishing connections between participants in stories, or between storyteller and audience, narrators articulate delicately, and often obliquely, the social networks at Iskut Village.

Arthur Nole 'glassing around' in the Skeena headwaters, August 2009.

Often, Iskut hunting stories do not take place at a specific or identifiable time in the past. I found this frustrating. But the narratives point to the historical past indirectly, and specific times are not always relevant. These stories are more likely to be generalized accounts of hunting episodes, like Arthur's story in the introduction. As such, they imply connections between past and present (also P. Moore 2007). Moreover, they are not myths and rarely occur in myth-time. They frequently, however, contain myth-like charters, or covenants, for interacting with animals. They sometimes refer discreetly to the power that animals have to control the outcome of hunts but do not usually transcend ordinary occurrences in hunters' lives. These conversational narratives are rather commonplace expressions of the importance of hunting. That is why they are hard to see as something special.

I tend to use the words 'narrative' and 'story' synonymously, though I acknowledge that this might not be true in all circumstances (Palmer

2005, 13).[13] When I ask them, Iskut people are not clear about the Tahltan word for 'story.' When I pressed her, elder Martha James says that *hedōn desi* means 'to tell a story.' Perhaps my questioning is imprecise, or respondents care little for such minutiae. Responding in an interview to a request for words relating to narratives, however, Robert Quock outlined some of the types of stories that Iskut people tell.[14] First, he identified *sa'e* stories as accounts of animals that interacted and communicated with humans before the Iskut encountered white people.[15] We can gloss *sa'e* as 'long time ago,' and storytellers use the label '*sa'e* story' to identify tales that take place in the distant past.[16] Notably, passing references to *sa'e* stories are more common than complete retellings of them. But why? Have they been forgotten? If the old stories have ceased to circulate, how do the rules about hunting survive? These questions motivate my work.[17]

Next, Robert identified historical narratives and offered examples of recent events, just out of living memory. *Bahi* 'war' stories are historical narratives, he said, about raids against neighbours, and he refers to the experiences of a Tahltan man, *Nākdił*, as an example.[18] Nisga'a people raided a Tahltan camp but found it empty because a woman there had heard them coming. *Nākdił*, the woman's husband, returned to the camp and on finding blood concluded that the Nisga'as had killed the woman. *Nākdił* sought revenge and killed a Nisga'a man. The story concludes with *Nākdił's* reconciliation with his Nisga'a victim's family (also Arthur Nole, personal communication, 23 August 2010).

Iskut people retell recent events as historical stories.[19] The most significant relate to guide outfitting and the guiding of client hunters on big-game hunts. Outfitter Tommy Walker is frequently the focus and sometimes the target of these accounts. Starting in 1948, Walker operated a business at *Hok'ats Łuwe Menh*. Many Tahltans worked for him during his twenty-four years in the business. Likewise, Robert explained that *hodi* means news – particularly bad news (also Arthur Nole, personal communication, 21 August 2009) – for example, reporting that someone has died. Other people in Iskut confirmed that *hodi* was news of death. *Hodi* actually means 'it is said' or 'they say,' and some Iskut say that it does not always connote bad news. One can speak of *hodi ti'e*, 'good news' (that which is said is good; *ti'e* means 'good'), although in this case, apparently, the speaker must mark *hodi* as good. In any case, *hodi* refers to the reporting of recent events, including sharing news about local hunts or driving trips.

Examples of Robert Quock's story types, listed above, appear in conversational narratives, although historical accounts of moose hunting and big-game guiding dominate my recordings. Like *hodi*, 'news,' hunting and guiding stories tell a great deal about the history of Iskut Village, its families, and their origins. They instruct young people how to treat food animals. They do not, however, have the cachet of myths in the village, in bureaucratic and legal circles, or even in anthropology. They do not have a pedigree in the *Journal of American Folklore*, as Teit's collection of Tahltan myth-time tales does (Teit 1919, 1921a, b).[20]

The repeated presence of narratives about hunting and history in conversations around Iskut suggests that people tell them in order to accomplish something (Schegloff 1997; Briggs 1993). I believe that these accounts assert that Iskut history is significant and relevant, particularly because of the otherwise marginal place of Iskut people in Canadian history and society. Community members convey in short form the details of events such as working with outfitter Tommy Walker in the 1950s and 1960s or moving from *Tlēgōhīn* to *Łuwechōn Menh* in the early 1960s. They share these tales with relatives, friends, and visitors who understand enough of the history to fill in the missing details. The stories circulate easily, but not without variation or debate, within the village. And they index (Peirce 1992, 5) – 'point to' – changing relationships with animals and outsiders. Iskut speakers thereby customize narratives about personal and group history, using them to rectify hurtful comments written by outsiders who do not understand them or share Iskut interests. Sometimes, these narratives identify the different versions of history that are known and shared within the village. In all these cases, the ethnography of speaking helps me to contextualize similar and divergent accounts of the past and of hunting in northern British Columbia.

The Ethnography of Hunting

Central to understanding hunting stories at Iskut is identifying relationships between hunters and their animal prey. A brief survey of the northern literature on this subject is helpful. Hallowell argues that relationships between the northern Ojibwe[21] and 'other than human' persons (animals) emulate social relations between people (1960, 21–22). Yet the Ojibwe kill animals for food but not usually each other. In *Hunters and Bureaucrats*, Nadasdy reiterates this position with reference to hunters of the southern Yukon. He asserts that Kluane hunters and their animal prey exhibit many of the same reciprocal commitments that people show to each other (Nadasdy 2003, 88, 94; also 2007). For the Kluanes, Ojibwe, and indeed Iskuts, animals are 'like people' and occasionally are people. As one might expect, then, these relationships create an ecology of life (Ingold 2000, 9–12) in which human relationships with animals pervade the extensive social networks that entangle all people (Nadasdy 2007, 31; also Anderson 2002; Blaser et al. 2010, 8).[22]

Other scholars of hunters and gatherers suggest that the ecological (and frequently economic) aspects and symbolic meanings of hunting permeate the lives of northern peoples (Shanklin 1985, 377). Algonkians, Crees, and Athapaskans assert that animals give themselves up as food to worthy hunters. Scholars write about this connection variously as a gift of animal to human (e.g., Ridington 1990b, 111, citing Sharp 1986), a love relationship (Preston 2002; Tanner 1979, 138), or a friendship deriving from myth-time (Tanner 1979, 136–40). They frequently characterize it as a sacrifice by an animal to people in need of sustenance (Speck 1945; Brightman 1993; Sharp 2001; also Martin 1978; more below). Humans maintain these relationships by acting 'respectfully' towards animals (Tanner 1979, 153–81; Ridington 1990b; Goulet 1998, 63–64; Nadasdy 2003, 83–94). The connections between animals and humans, however one characterizes them, are predictable: a hunter must treat animals properly because hunting traditions and mythology say as much. Failure to do so results in misfortune, failed hunts, and starvation. These hunter-prey relationships contrast starkly with the way in which many non-Native people, such as sports hunters, think about animals. For them, it is a right to kill animals because animals lack sentience (e.g., Loo 2001a, b).[23]

The notion of animal sacrifice is powerful. Building from Hubert and Mauss's analysis (Hubert and Mauss 1964 [1898]), Brightman says that the significance of animals' sacrifice to hungry humans derives from their role in mediating between the sacred and the profane realms of life (Brightman 1993, 224). The image of a sacrifice unites the utilitarian aspects of food-gathering with religious reverence for food animals. The animals provide themselves, their meat, as a gift to humans who – in an act of communion – celebrate them by eating them. By extension, the communion venerates the deities responsible for providing them to humans in the first place. *Etsen' Ma'*, the Meat Mother in Tahltan mythology, is one such deity (e.g., Teit 1919, 230–32). She is a widespread figure throughout Subarctic cultures (Cruikshank 1990). Elder Sophia Stanton described to me her role among the Iskut people: 'All kinds of animals born from [her] ... Now it's all as far as I know that *Etsen' Ma* make everything.' *Etsen' Ma* controls the flow of game to Iskut hunters. To upset her means certain starvation.

Relationships between hunters and their prey also present a series of dichotomies (Brightman 1993, 228–29; also Sharp 1994). Animals are sacrificial victims and benevolent benefactors. They control the outcome of hunts by choosing to sacrifice themselves to respectful hunters. They are dangerous because of their power over people, but if humans treat them properly, they are giving, caring, and loving of their human predators (Nadasdy 2005, 304). People receive animals and take them. Animals dominate the lives of humans, who in turn must kill them to survive. Humans are friends with them, but sometimes use coercion or trickery to kill them (also Tanner 1979, 148). Thus animals' dominance and control over humans become submission to the eventual assertiveness of hunters. In all of this, there is an exchange that must continue for the animals to fulfil their purpose, for humans to eat, and for deities such as *Etsen' Ma'* to remain happy. In this mutual dependence, animals receive veneration and people receive sustenance. 'If the hunter fails to live up to his or her reciprocal obligations toward animals . . . the animals may exact spiritual retribution, causing misfortune, sickness, or even death' (Nadasdy 2005, 304). Sacrifice by animals for the benefit of humans comes with very real costs to animals and humans alike.

Tahltan mythology, variations of which circulate at Iskut, describes animals' punishment of thoughtless or careless hunters (Teit 1919, 1921a, b). Still, I only rarely heard Iskut people say that animals give themselves up to respectful hunters. No one explained to me what it meant to show respect to animals even when I asked directly.[24] My academic expectations, which I detailed above, did not correspond with the reality of the village life and hunting activities that I witnessed. I did, however, find myself frequently participating in indirect talk about people being respectful towards animals and meat at Iskut. For example, elders warned me not to be stingy with the fish I caught or with everyday items such as my cassette tapes – as if to say that I should share these items with them. And instead of hearing about animals in myth-time stories, I heard many accounts of people hunting, working as hunting guides, and butchering animals. Much of this talk included allusions to punishment by animals.

Humans' intermediary role between sacrificial animals and venerated deities also is different today from in the past. Hunters receive animal as gifts, but recent Catholic traditions in the village suggest that some, if not all, hunters respect the Catholic God. As Arthur Nole says, '[I] pray to the Lord' after each kill. Likewise, elder Sophia Stanton explains that *Tsesk'iye Chō,* 'Big Crow,' the Tahltan transformer and culture hero, is actually Jesus Christ.[25] Moreover, spoken references to reciprocal connections between animals and humans may omit mention of deities. In these cases, older themes and expressions of respect remain, but the exchange exists between hunter and prey only. To be sure, some Iskut people might not interpret relations between hunter and prey as Arthur and Sophia do (also Feit 2004, 106).

Newer hunting activities also allow for novel deviations from the original hunter-prey system. The guiding of non-Native hunters on hunts for trophy and sport, hence hunting for a wage, constitutes one example. In this case, the animal's gift becomes a commodity (Tanner 1979, 11; also Nadasdy 2007). Villagers sell that commodity and receive cash as the reward for their labour. Rather than the animal's offering itself up to the hunter, the hunter-as-labourer 'takes' it. When Iskut people talk about animal-human relationships in terms of commodities or Catholicism, they may be directing audiences away from major cultural themes that they consider private or inappropriate for government studies. Likewise, such talk does not negate capitalistic interests or blaspheme Catholic beliefs. And, depending on circumstance and audience, artful and careful talk of human-animal relationships creates distance from hunting for Iskut people, lest listeners perceive it as the work of poor people or acquire a strong and positive image of a contemporary person who embraces ties to older practices (also Loo 2006, 58).

The Politics of Hunting

More than an ethnography of contemporary hunting, this book provides an example of the politics of hunting in Canada.[26] Hunting at Iskut Village takes place increasingly in the context of resource development by companies like Shell Canada and Fortune Minerals. Shell Canada owns the rights to explore for coal-bed methane in the *Tl'abāne,* and Fortune Minerals owns the coal leases on *Dzełtsedle;* both projects are located in the heart of Iskut camping and hunting grounds. The reactions of Iskut people and other Tahltans to these projects have been direct and confrontational. Between 2005 and 2008, blockades, Internet campaigns, collaborations with environmentalists, and court actions have been launched in an effort to prevent development in the

Tl'abāne. In a Master's thesis, Ellen Morgan dissects the conflict between Iskut hunters and resource companies (Morgan 2009). She argues that the conflict over resources in the *Tl'abāne*, known now locally and in environmental circles as the Sacred Headwaters, is a direct result of neo-liberal policies of the British Columbia government (23; also Davis 2011b). These policies include a generous mineral staking and tenuring process that has promoted exploration and mining development over the rights of Aboriginal peoples to consultation regarding activities on traditional lands.

The politics of hunting at Iskut Village forms a subtext for this book. Drawing inspiration from Morgan's research, and from Harvey Feit's observation that the impact of neo-liberalism on the practices of Aboriginal peoples has received little attention (Feit 2010, 49), I argue that the hunting practices of Iskut people must be understood in terms of their history and experiences with wage work and capitalism. I describe first hunting in the era of fur trading and guiding prior to the 1970s. Iskut people participated widely in the inland fur trade up until the 1950s. While fur trading did not stop completely at that time, Iskut people eagerly embraced outfitting and big-game guiding in the 1950s and 1960s.[27] Both fur trading and guiding provided Iskut people with work in which they controlled their labour, the products of their labour, and to a large extent the level to which non-Native fur traders and outfitters were successful. This mirrors the observations of scholars like Feit (2010), Micheal Asch (1982) and Adrian Tanner (1979) who, observing other parts of northern Native Canada, note that the trade in furs in the first half of the twentieth century represented a mercantilist period in which the neo-local was embraced by Natives on local terms (Feit 2010, 52). For Asch, the fur trade in the Northwest Territories worked effectively because of indigenous knowledge of the animals and land (Asch 1982, 362). For Tanner, the fur trade in northern Quebec was successful because Native people operated autonomously (Tanner 1979, xiii). Trade relations are central to the practices of commercial hunting and guiding, and these practices do not change fundamental social relationships between Natives or between Natives and their non-Native commercial partners (Feit 2010, 56). At Iskut, stories of the sustenance hunt (Chapter 3) and of guiding (Chapter 4) echo the experiences of Natives in the Northwest Territories and Quebec. In the Iskut accounts, relationships with animals remain predicated on age-old covenants with animals. Accounts of the relationships between Iskut guides and non-Native outfitters like Tommy Walker and Steele Hyland also exhibit the characteristics of confrontation and respect.

I describe a second and more recent era of resource development and exploitation beginning about 1960. It is marked by the loss of control and a limited role for Iskut families and, at times, their elected leaders in decision-making about the extraction of resources like minerals and furs.[28] By the 1960s, Iskut families were living at what is now Iskut Village. Located near *Łuwechōn Menh*, Iskut people chose to move to this old camping spot and establish a village with the assistance of the Department of Indian Affairs because they wanted to be closer to traplines on the Spatsizi Plateau and in the *Tl'abāne* (Chapter 2). But the move paralleled an increasing dissociation from the land and sustenance hunting. Highway 37 was built in the 1960s and early 1970s, linking Iskut first to the Alaska Highway and then to the highways of southern British Columbia; cargo on trucks followed, as did tourists. British Columbia Railway (henceforth BC Rail) began work on its railway extension to *Tatl'ah*. Mines and miners were sure to follow, but railway construction was halted in the mid-1970s and never resumed because of funding problems and scandal (Sheppard 1983b, 249). By the mid-1980s, Gulf Oil was removing coal from *Dzełtsedle*, but that project was unprofitable and short-lived. With Shell Canada's recent acquisition of the coal-bed methane rights and Fortune Minerals' ownership of the coal rights, *Dzełtsedle* and the *Tl'abāne* are under threat of extensive development again. Iskut people have been challenged to protest the developments and the lack of control they represent. An unregulated, non-Native hunt in the *Tl'abāne* provoked another blockade in the fall of 2009; new hunting regulations were introduced in 2010 as a result. The protests of the past five years indicate that Iskut people feel they have shared the land enough with non-Natives and the profiteers of British Columbia's resource-driven economy (cf. Feit 2004, 97). At the very least, Iskut people want a say in how or if local lands are developed.

But the demand for the minerals in the *Tl'abāne* has also opened up new avenues for Iskut people to assert their indigenous rights (Morgan 2009, 29). Iskut people have chosen traditional use and traditional knowledge studies as one means of engaging the development process directly (this chapter). Chief Louie's public speech at an old outfitting camp in 2004 (Chapter 5) provides an example of the political rhetoric that Iskut politicians draw on to assert claims to land, history, and family identity. Resistance strategies, like blockades and court challenges, are discussed in Chapter 6. The sacredness alluded to in the Sacred Headwaters moniker, now used to refer to the *Tl'abāne*, rejects the commodification of the land and animals in favour of a worldview that insists that people, the land, and animals co-exist and are related to each other in an intricate web of life (Ingold 2000, 24–25). Further, and to paraphrase Blaser et al., the processes of globalization reconstitute relations among people and between people and other living beings (2010, 9). Globalization reconfigures intimate social relationships to the material and commodity focuses of economics and politics. In their own political actions, predicated on their personal connections to land and animals, Iskut families are pushing back. This is what it means, increasingly, to be *didene*. To exploit the land, to treat it without respect, is akin to treating animals that way; punishment is bound to follow (also Anderson 2002, 117). The Iskut experience of sustenance hunting and the images of hunting as noble, traditional, or impoverished play out both historically and today in front of these complex sets of national and international demands.

My Position and an Outline of the Study

Over the years, I have found several roles for myself at Iskut, and they have allowed me greater access to some areas of village life than to others. I developed associations with the elders, usually adults over the age of fifty-five, and spent a great deal of time socializing in their circles and assisting many of them with daily activities such as shovelling snow and chopping wood. The elders appreciated this role of helper, and the political leadership in the village accepted it. The health-care staff at the village clinic encouraged my involvement and understood the value of regular social activities for the oldest residents. It was a safe position for me, as it allowed me to form meaningful relationships with people who, like elder Martha James, did not find a young man who wanted to spend long periods travelling with them or visiting at their homes socially threatening. For the most part, however, I worked closely with older men and recorded more of their stories than those of women. I did work with a few older women, but less intensively, because it was impractical and inappropriate for me to camp with women. I experienced life in Iskut as a young man, to paraphrase Brody (2000, 5), and my research both benefits and suffers from gender and age imbalances.

As is common with ethnographic projects, I worked intensively with a small group of people who were knowledgeable about the topics I was researching. More specifically, I worked closely with six elders. Most of these people were widows or widowers and, as it turned out, did not drive, were unable to drive, or did not own a vehicle. I spent much of my time with them driving around the village and local countryside, talking about the places that we were seeing, conducting interviews as we drove, taking pictures, and recording general conversations. I asked for fishing lessons in exchange for rides to the lake. I tagged along on hunting expeditions because I had a truck. I embraced the role of driver most of the time because it gave me opportunities to talk with people individually and to learn about Iskut places. It was an expensive means of conducting research because of the high price of gasoline at Iskut. The demands of driving around the area and to visit my family in Vancouver meant that I logged about 20,000 miles during my thirteen months of research. Having grown up in the city and lacking mechanical skills to speak of, I learned to maintain my truck and how to change the oil, which I did regularly in the garage of my duplex in the village.[29]

I accepted a nominal and unpaid position in the Iskut First Nation's political headquarters – the 'band office' – a utilitarian building in the centre of the reserve. I became an unofficial member of the 'band staff' and assisted with cultural projects and other tasks when an extra hand was necessary. This position was natural for me. I was already familiar with the band office and its staff from my time assisting with the Traditional Use Study, and I enjoyed the work; it gave me an intimate understanding of how the band office operated and allowed me to serve as note-taker and occasional researcher.

Although these activities and events might appear peripheral to documenting hunting practices, managing local lands and relations with resource companies and government officials allow some Iskut people to continue with hunting traditions. The work in the band office also gave me a place to go when the older people with whom I worked were busy elsewhere. My position in the community was marginal, as is that of most anthropologists, and people rarely interrupted their lives to seek me out. Instead, I tried to join in when I saw that activities were taking place.

I have returned to Iskut almost every year since I completed my dissertation research in 2002. Some of those trips were recreational, others emerged from my continuing participation in land-use planning with the Iskut First Nation and the Tahltan Central Council. Sometimes my role in land-planning processes merged in intriguing ways with my academic interests in hunting. In the winter of 2008, it shocked me to hear a government representative ask in a meeting why Iskut Tahltans could not simply move their hunting camps out of the mineral-rich areas of their territory. That question prompted me to conduct a small ethnographic study of camps and camping during the summer of 2009.[30] Since 2005, I have watched protests at Iskut against Shell Canada and other resource-extraction companies from my home in North Vancouver. Three years of resistance by some Iskut leaders led to the initiation in 2008 of a two-year moratorium against exploration. In all, I have continued to consider the importance of hunting and its expressions on the land, like camps and stories, in ways that challenge the reifying objectives of traditional use and traditional knowledge studies.

I present this book in six chapters and an introduction. The introduction establishes the tone and substance of Iskut talk about hunting with the short, characteristic hunting narrative by Arthur Nole. The situation in which he tells his story is also representative of the new contexts – a school classroom in this case – in which people talk about hunting and the past. Chapters 1 and 2 (Part I) present the background to the conversational narratives that illustrate chapters 3, 4, and 5 (Part II). Chapter 2 is historical. I show how, during the twentieth century, Iskut individuals and families interacted with outsiders and engaged in mercantilist practices in ways that allowed them to maintain sustenance hunting practices. Sure, guiding and trapping resulted in a cash wage, but both activities fit within the general worldview of sustenance hunters. Further, I suggest that what resembles an Iskut ethnic group today formed slowly during the twentieth century after several moves between permanent village sites. Smaller nuclear families and hunting groups combined and recombined, culminating in the consolidation of Iskut families at Iskut Village. This is the common history of the Iskut families. But Iskut people debate and contest this history regularly. On inspection, we learn that there is no single history for Iskut people. I also include a sketch of life in Iskut Village as I experienced it in 2002 and 2003.

Part II presents examples of hunting talk and its contexts. These chapters show that diverse personal and family histories complicate definitions of the Iskut group. And, together, the chapters follow a shift in hunting outlooks in Iskut. They move from the discussion of sustenance hunting and relations with moose in chapter 3, to an account of guiding activities in chapter 4, to the overt invocation of a hunting heritage in a political speech in chapter 5. This shift parallels the arrival and evolving impact of mercantile and capitalist resource-extraction activities in Iskut hunting territories.

More specifically, chapter 3 describes the relationships between hunters and their prey. I present the rules for humans interacting with food animals and investigate the ways in which people treat animals today. I also analyse the talk of hunters remembering past hunts to show that old ideas about animals often underlie and inform hunting talk. In chapter 4, I turn to the role of domesticated animals, particularly dogs and horses, in Iskut life. I offer the transcript of Robert Quock's accounts of his experiences working with horses for non-Native outfitter Tommy Walker. The stories show how work animals, and the history of wage work more generally, are an allegory for cultural change. In chapter 5, I turn to an example of the elected Iskut chief discussing his people's history overtly. In July 2004, amid great celebrations, Iskut people in northwestern British Columbia 'returned home' to a former camp in the village's hinterland. There Chief Louie welcomed Iskut families and non-Native guests with a speech in which he reflected on Iskut alienation from traditional lands and the historical inaccuracies that appear in non-Native history books. His address shows how Iskut people use the past to debate the political and economic changes that have followed outside interventions. And it presents the sophisticated use by Chief Louie of a moribund ethnonym – a little-used ethnic label – in response to local arguments about tradition in a new era of resource development. Once again, Tommy Walker lurks in the background.

In chapter 6, I bring the story of Iskut economic changes to the present by addressing the recent blockades against Shell Canada and Fortune Minerals. In an era of resource exploration and development in northern British Columbia, talking respectfully about animals is analogous to acting respectfully towards the land. I conclude that hunting provides Iskut people with the most powerful way of expressing who they are. In all these chapters, my focus lies where Iskut interests do: on the stories and memories that Iskut people deploy strategically when interacting with each other and with non-Native people.

2 Iskut History and Hunting

During the summer of 2000, I visited Iskut Village to make arrangements for my dissertation research. While there, I also helped with genealogical documentation in the cultural research office of the Iskut First Nation. As that work progressed, I noticed that the screen saver on the office's computer read: 'Susan and Mary are the proudest Bear Lakers there ever was.' First cousins Susan Knox and Mary Folke are Iskut community members and paid cultural researchers. Knowing something of the peripatetic history of the people now living at Iskut Village, I did not find the scrolling statement strange. I recognized, however, its overt acknowledgment of the connections of some Iskut families to Bear Lake, British Columbia, home to Fort Connolly, a former post of the Hudson's Bay Company. With their telling phrase, Susan and Mary asserted their links to an area where, according to the academic literature about northern Athapaskans, people speak the Dakelh (Carrier) and Sekani languages. With no mention of Tahltans, the words on the computer screen challenged Iskut connections with other Tahltan speakers who lived at *Tlēgōhīn* and *Tatl'ah*. They also bespoke the energy of Iskut people's efforts to define themselves independently from their relatives at *Tlēgōhīn*.[1]

By not using the label 'Iskut,' Mary and Susan's phrase reminded me how recent a name Iskut is. The word Iskut may be of Nisga'a origin (Akrigg and Akrigg 1997, 123). Local people use it because their village is in the headwaters of the Iskut River; the Iskut River meets the Stikine River downstream from *Tlēgōhīn*. As an ethnic marker, Iskut does not have much ethnographic or historical significance. Yet the community and Iskut people individually refer proudly to themselves as the Iskut First Nation and Iskut people. In doing so, they do not call on any family, single hunting territory, or even a large Native group to stand for the people who live at Iskut. In a similar fashion, the Iskut Village itself is an anomaly in their history. Although some families have lived at the site for a long time, the village as it is today dates from 1962.

The screen-saver phrase left me uncertain about who at Iskut claims an Iskut ethnicity. Had the idea of an Iskut ethnicity existed in the past, and if so how does that history, that origin story, manifest itself today? The screen saver reminds me now that there is no single Iskut hunting tradition. Various hunting experiences and opportunities for wage work inform individual, family, and village ideas about what it means to be an Iskut person. Sometimes the community presents a single Iskut identity publicly. Iskut people present themselves during some political negotiations, for example, as culturally and historically distinct from their Tahltan-speaking relatives and neighbours at *Tlēgōhīn* and from other Canadians. Yet when they need strength in numbers, they embrace associations with neighbours, Native and not. And in still other instances, stories that families tell – which include references to places such as Bear Lake – permeate conversations and create a number of smaller hunting and historical communities within Iskut Village. Hunting is the common thread.

Three themes in the twentieth-century history of Iskut people and their village near *Łuwechōn Menh* stand out. First, participation in both sustenance hunting and wage work dominates the recent history. The ancestors of today's Iskut families moved in and out of a wage economy constantly, but sporadically, throughout the century. Sustenance hunting and fishing remained a significant economic activity for most Iskut people before 1962. After this date, wage work in the construction of northern infrastructure and trophy hunting supplemented, but did not eliminate, the bush economy. The gradual shift from sustenance hunting to wage work, and the continuing interplay of both activities today, is traced through this book in the stories Iskut people tell.[2]

Second, Iskut families have moved frequently, but never aimlessly, in the past one hundred years, including seasonal rounds from villages to camps and back, with families relocating into and out of the now 'traditional territory.' Some relocated their primary villages from places such as Caribou Hide[3] and *Me'etsendāne* to *Tlēgōhīn* and *Łuwechōn Menh*, the site of Iskut Village today. Some people went to new sites in pursuit of new wage opportunities and game or at the encouragement of Indian agents and missionaries. Not all families stayed together, however, and these relocations usually did not mean lasting commitments to particular places or specific wage employment. The movements anchor Iskut traditions to a series of homes and a network of trails and indeed to hunting itself. They emphasize changes in sustenance hunting, with long walking trips, for example, giving way to shorter, driving trips.[4]

Third, and because of frequent moves, Iskut families have lived together in a number of combinations. The result is the heterogeneous make up of the village today. Iskut talk suggests that the varying composition of the village is a source of both internal strength and conflict. Some family groups find themselves vying for political standing and thus formal responsibility for interacting with outsiders. Others act as a single community, confronting challenges flowing from their association with neighbouring Aboriginal and non-Aboriginal groups. The village's diverse composition also leads to various expressions of traditional ecological knowledge. When speaking Tahltan, some families use Sekani names for fish and animals; other families use Tahltan names. Each family has experienced the local physical environment somewhat differently. Once families decided to settle permanently at Iskut, hunting formed the constant in people's otherwise disparate experiences.

Iskut in the Twentieth Century

Social Groupings

Before developing further the three themes in recent Iskut history – a shifting combination of hunting and wage work, frequent moves, and group recombinations – it is helpful to identify the social groups that appear in that story. These groups appear to be simply families. Visitors to Iskut sometimes remark, for example, on the apparent family connections between everyone in the village. They identify these links through the patronyms that dominate rolls of village members; a glance at the acknowledgments to this book testifies to this reality. But patronyms do not reveal the full story of social and ancestral connections. Bilateral ties through marriage and partnerships of friends – *pāne*, 'partner' – are just as important (Lanoue 1992, 78–90).

Lack of precise definitions of family and group in Iskut and in Athapaskan anthropology complicate the analysis of the history of Iskut families in the first half of the twentieth century.[5] Because many Iskut people as well as academics assert that at least some ancestors of Iskut residents are Sekanis (e.g., Jenness 1937; MacLachlan 1981;

Sheppard 1983b, 299; Lanoue 1992), Lanoue's analysis of Sekani groups offers a point of departure. In *Brothers,* Lanoue accepts in part Helm's distinctions between local and regional bands – a 'local band is composed of one or more domestic groups or nuclear families that is structurally equivalent to the hunting group' (Lanoue 1992, 141; cf. Helm 1965). The social organization of Iskut's ancestors was almost certainly akin to that of late-eighteenth-century local bands or hunting groups. But Lanoue is not sure that any rigid definition of group membership is meaningful for the Sekani until the 1960s and the flooding of Williston Lake behind the W.A.C. Bennett Dam (Lanoue 1992, 141). The creation of Iskut Village in 1962 is a similar, group-defining event for Iskut people. I propose that pragmatic considerations have shaped membership in hunting, trading, and wage-working arrangements. Iskut ancestral families could form and re-form larger groups in any number of combinations, depending on members' needs.[6]

Yet Iskut people themselves talk today in terms of ancestral families or groups of families largely on the basis of patriarchs who have patronyms that are the same as their own. They speak proudly of ancestors such as Antoine Louie and Old Dennis, patriarchs of small groups of closely related adults and children. Moreover, the politics of land and resource claims is encouraging the revival of older ethnonyms – group names associated with hunting territories (chapter 5). In both cases – that of small patronymic family groups and somewhat larger ethnonymic groups – boundaries are emerging between nuclear and extended (i.e., multi-generational) families. In these situations, support for the election of relatives to political posts or the assertion of rights to hunting territories and campsites supersedes village unity.[7]

Thus flexible membership complicates definitions of family and ethnic groups at Iskut (e.g., Sheppard 1983b, 274, 299, 329). At different times during the year and periods in their lives, people affiliate variously with the family of their birth, with their in-laws, and with friends – hardly surprising. In my discussion of Iskut history, then, I will use the relatively transparent notion that nuclear families in the village today, which identify and group themselves into larger extended families by patronyms, associate themselves with specific hunting territories and camps on the Spatsizi Plateau, in the *Tl'abāne,* and elsewhere. This is what I see and hear Iskut people doing to identify themselves – except when they talk about themselves in ways that make these transparent groups meaningless!

The Physical Setting

Iskut Village sits in a narrow river valley filled with a series of lakes that form the headwaters of the Iskut River (Figure 3). It is closest to lakes *Łuwechōn* and *Edōnetenajān* which are both excellent spots for catching *tsabā'e* / *deghai*, 'rainbow trout,' with rods or through the ice. Depending on whom you talk to and where they come from, the Tahltan language calls rainbow trout (*Oncorhynchus mykiss*) variously *tsabā'e* or *deghai*.[8] The village sits in the afternoon shadow of,a large mountain rising 4,000 feet above the valley floor; from it juts a rock formation called *Tuhtseyghuda'* that looks like the beak of a loon. To the east, gentle hills covered in poplar trees rise to elevations beyond which trees no longer grow because of cold winter temperatures and snow. Iskut residents appreciate these aesthetic qualities. They enjoy surveying the surrounding hills for animals particularly in September, when the leaves of *k'is* ('mountain alder,' *Alnus incana*) turn a brilliant yellow.

The upper Iskut River valley lies between the temperate, wet Coast Mountains and the extreme temperature variations of the interior cordillera. In 2002 and 2003, when I lived in Iskut, winter temperatures at the village (elevation 900 m or 3,000 feet) ranged between −10°C and −35°C (14°F and −31°F), with several feet of snow falling between October and April. The summertime weather patterns included hot sun, frequent rain, and temperatures between 10°C and 32°C (50°F and 90°F). The region boasts several major river systems and includes the headwaters of the Iskut, *Hok'āz Tū'e* (Klappan), Nass, Skeena, and Stikine rivers.[9] The five species of Pacific salmon in the Stikine cannot reach the upper Stikine watershed because of obstructions on the Stikine and Iskut rivers, and their absence (except in the upper Skeena watershed) reinforces the Iskut orientation towards hunting. As with other Arctic-watershed Athapaskans, the preference for hunting big game over fishing distinguishes Iskut Tahltans from *Tlēgōhīn* Tahltans. Indeed, a more flexible sense of group membership and territorial delineation, as we saw above, may also result from this focus away from the Pacific Ocean towards the interior at Iskut.[10]

Iskut people gather food and find recreation in several physiographical regions with elevations below 1,400 m (4,500 feet), tree-lined river valleys, and diverse vegetation, where they harvest medicines and some wild vegetables. The forests also provide the *gāza* (locally the 'jack pine'; lodgepole pine, *Pinus contorta*; see Turner 1997, 1998: 90–91; Carter, Carlick, and Carlick 1994, 180), *chabā'e* ('poplar,' *Populus*

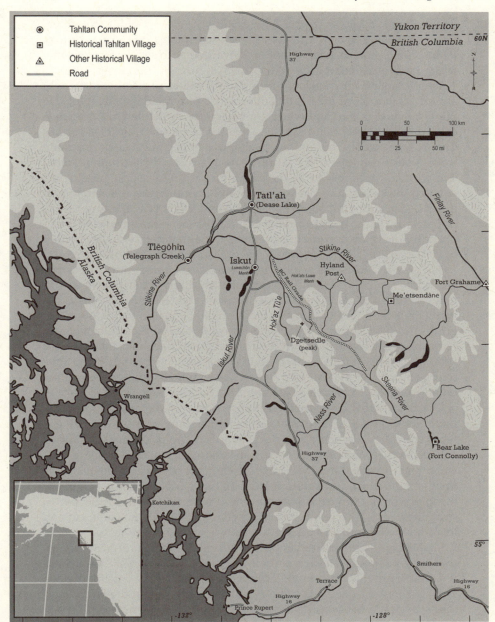

Northwestern British Columbia. Map by Bill Angelbeck.

tremuloides, P. trichocarpa, and *P. balsamifera*), and *k'is* ('mountain alder,' *Alnus tenuifolia*), which villagers use to heat their homes or to smoke meat year round. The abundant *kedā* ('moose,' *Alces alces*) is the staple of the traditional Iskut diet.

The food-gathering seasonal round takes Iskut people onto large sub-alpine plateau lands located south and east of the village. Much of this land is *tl'abāne*, meaning open, grassy flat land, which led to the historical group name *Tl'abānot'ine*.[11] Descendant families of the *Tl'abānot'ine* live in Iskut today and evoke that label occasionally to differentiate themselves from *Tl'ogot'ine*, 'Long Grass,' families.[12] Starting in August and continuing through much of the autumn, Iskut people hunt in the valley of *Hok'āz Tū'e* and in the headwaters of the Spatsizi River. Moose remain plentiful here, and Iskut and non-Iskut people alike hunt them by truck along the trackless rail bed of BC Rail's never-completed line.[13] These highland areas contain extensive grazing ranges for a large herd of *hodzih* ('caribou,' *Rangifer tarandus osborni*). Also common to this area, and popular with Iskut food gatherers, are *dechuwe* ('porcupines,' *Erethizon dorsatum nigrescens*), *dediye* ('groundhogs'; marmots, *Marmota monax petrensis* or *Marmota caligata*), *gah* ('rabbit'; snowshoe hare, *Lepus americanus macfarlani*), *tsa'* ('beaver,' *Castor canadensis sagittatus*), and *tsili* ('gophers'; ground squirrels, *Spermophilus undulates plesius*). The mountainsides are home to a protected species of *debehe* ('sheep,' *Ovis dalli stonei*) and to *isbā* ('mountain goat,' *Oreamnos americanus columbiae*). These white goats love to roll in the red, mineral-rich sands of the Spatsizi Plateau; hence the name Spatsizi – a contraction of *isbā*, 'goat,' and *detsīdzi*, 'red.'

The lakes in this area contain several species of fish. Iskut people comment, for example, that *Hok'ats Łuwe Menh* contains a majority of the regional freshwater species, including *deghati / ło* ('whitefish,' *Prosopium williamsoni, P. cylindraceum*, or *Coregonus clupeaformis*), *hostlose* ('ling cod,' sometimes burbot, *Lota lota*), *tāshde* ('Arctic grayling,' *Thymallus arcticus*), *tsabā'e* ('lake trout,' *Salvelinus namaycush*), and *tsabā'e / deghai* ('rainbow trout,' *Oncorhynchus mykiss*). *Łuwechōn Menh*, a few hundred metres from Iskut Village, is full of *tsabā'e / deghai*, 'rainbow trout,' and rod and ice fishers use it reliably throughout the year. In the recent past, people ice-fished here and elsewhere with nets under the ice or with snares that they dropped through the ice on cords. Notably, Tahltan speakers fish mainly on the divide between the Arctic and Pacific oceans. Thus people at Iskut have some familiarity with fish in the two watersheds and mix fish names; some people call whitefish by its *Tlēgōhīn* (coastal) name, *deghati*, and others use the interior (Arctic) form, *ło*.

A Sketch of Iskut in 2002

Iskut Village is on BC Highway 37, 'the Stewart-Cassiar Highway,' about 350 km (215 miles) south of Watson Lake, a town on the Alaska Highway in Yukon (Figure 4). This road reached Iskut in 1976 and now runs north from Kitwanga, a Gitksan village, to the BC-Yukon border. Many tourists and truckers use it to avoid the Alaska Highway en route from the continental United States to Alaska.

Iskut Village looks like a suburb, with about a hundred houses in two main areas around a series of cul-de-sacs and an arterial road. Most of the homes there now were built in the late 1980s and early 1990s. Demand for reserve housing has increased in recent years. Twenty new houses were built in 2006 and three more were constructed in 2010. Some older log buildings also serve as houses or as warehouses (sheds) for equipment relating to cutting wood, hunting, snowshoeing, or tobogganing. The band office, school, store, and outdoor hockey rink are all in the centre of the village. The Iskut Clinic, a nursing station with a staff of Native and non-Native caregivers, is near the Catholic church and rectory on the south side of *Setū* Creek. This small brook splits the village in two, separating most homes on the north side from the former camping sites, the first band office, and now the health clinic.

The village has about 350 residents, perhaps 20 of them outsiders teaching in the school or working in the clinic. All homes and services are within walking distance of one another, although most people drive from place to place. Extended families and adult siblings tend to live in houses close to one another, usually on the same street or cul-de-sac. This preference for living near siblings is an old pattern and possibly derives from early times, when the primary measure of affiliation was the matrilineal family (Hawkes 1966; Adlam 1985).

The dirt roads linking parts of the village are heavily travelled by pickups, four-wheel all-terrain vehicles (ATVs, or 'bikes'), snowmobiles, graders, and other work vehicles. Mud encrusts all of them, and the many broken windshields testify to the loose gravel. Away from the main village roads, trails snake through the trees behind houses and provide access to backyards by foot, bike, or snowmobile. Many Iskut yards are meticulously tidy, and most have woodpiles stacked high. Children's bicycles and toys or an old car clutter some yards.

Small campsites behind many houses replicate bush camps outside the village. They have picnic tables, sheds, large firepits for cooking meat, and, in many cases, smokehouses for smoking fish and meat. The

Houses near the centre of Iskut Village. *Łuwechōn Menh* is at the toe of the mountain, behind the village. The old trail to *Tlēgōhīn* runs through the gap in the top right corner of the photograph.

domestic camps illustrate residents' need to work on hides, cut and cure meat or fish, and store equipment for extended camping trips. Many families also keep *tlī'*, 'dogs,' which typically live outside in the yards all year. Dogs have been valuable work animals for hunting families in the recent past, and they continue to be companions and, at times, objects of scorn for the care they require (chapter 4). Other animals are visible in the village too. *Tsesk'iye*, 'crow or raven,' are common throughout the year. Occasionally *sas*, 'bear,' or *nusihe*, 'foxes,' appear in the village, but large grazing animals such as *kedā*, 'moose,' are rare.

Iskut people are influenced culturally by Tlingits on the Pacific coast to the west and Sekani-speaking Athapaskans in the Rocky Mountain Trench to the east (Dawson 1888; Emmons 1911; Teit 1917; Jenness 1937). The use of black-and-red button blankets and assertions of clan affiliations remain Iskut Villagers' most obvious connections with peoples of the northwest coast. Iskut people affiliate with either the *Tsesk'iye*,

'Crow,' or the *Chi'yōne*, 'Wolf,' clan and trace their membership through their mother's family. These matrilineal ties are particularly important at funerals, when membership determines specific roles and responsibilities. People are aware of clan groups when they date, and marriage preferences continue to show exogamous patterns. In other village activities, however, clan membership is less central. Seating at community dinners is, for example, by choice; other preferences, including friendship, may apply instead.

From the Remembered Past to the Lived Present

Participation in sustenance hunting and extensive wage-based hunting and guiding has affected families and extended family groups during their tenure in three permanent communities: Caribou Hide and *Me'etsendāne*, neighbouring villages used consecutively and located east of the current village on the Spatsizi Plateau (1910s–1940s); the 'Commonage' at *Tlēgōhīn* (1950s); and the current village site at Iskut, near *Łuwechōn Menh* (1960s–present). While *Me'etsendāne* and the Commonage no longer have residents, buildings remain at both places.

Twentieth-century movements paralleled decreasing reliance on sustenance food gathering and increasing participation in wage-earning activities like guiding and road construction, culminating in 1962 in the consolidation of families who consider themselves Iskut people into a single and permanent village. But the story of this consolidation, presented below, suggests that Iskut people have always adapted to changing circumstances and embraced new opportunities. It points to the flexibility of sustenance practices and the ease with which people integrated new wage-earning opportunities with traditional knowledge and economic systems. Although every family experienced these moves differently, travel through much of northern British Columbia is part of the collective history that Iskut people draw on when asserting a unified ethnic identity.

Caribou Hide and Me'etsendāne *(1910s–1940s)*

The oldest Iskut residents, and the ancestors of many Iskut people, lived with their extended families at the village of *Me'etsendāne* between 1922 and 1948. In the decade or so prior to this, the families dwelled nearby at the village of Caribou Hide. *Me'etsendāne* and Caribou Hide are 24 km (15 miles) apart. Both places are a walk of several days east of present-day Iskut Village. The arrival of Iskut ancestors and others at *Me'etsendāne* exemplifies the frequent movements of people through-out northern British Columbia at the turn of the twentieth century. A group of Native people, probably Sekani speakers, was living at Fort Connolly, the Hudson's Bay Company's post at Bear Lake, when it closed in the 1890s. After that, the 'Bear Lake Indians' moved north into the Spatsizi Plateau.[14] According to Sheppard, they met two Tahltan bands, the *Tl'ogot'ine* and the *Tl'abānot'ine*, in the Spatsizi and *Tl'abāne* regions respectively.[15] The three groups amalgamated at Caribou Hide (Sheppard 1983b, 335; Friesen 1985, 30–32; Jenness 1937, 13–15; Lanoue 1992, 153). MacLachlan adds that some of the Bear Lake people migrated to Fort Grahame and Fort Ware on the Finlay River before moving to Caribou Hide. Thus, people sometimes apply the label 'Fort Grahame Nomads' to Iskut residents, too. Plans for a mine in the area, MacLachlan says, encouraged the move to Caribou Hide (MacLachlan 1956, 36).[16]

Caribou Hide and *Me'etsendāne* served as a base for sustenance hunt-ing and commercial trapping and guiding throughout the Spatsizi Plateau. Both villages had central locations along a well-worn trail that stretched between the Hudson's Bay post at *Tlēgōhīn*, on the navigable lower Stikine River, and Fort Grahame, and later Fort Ware, along the Finlay River. *Tlēgōhīn* and *Me'etsendāne* were about 150 miles apart, and someone on foot carrying a heavy load might have needed more than a week to travel between the two places. Because of these distances, and the groups' interior hunting orientation, it seems likely that hunters vis-ited Fort Connolly and Fort Grahame more regularly than *Tlēgōhīn*. In 1922, influenza struck the groups living at Caribou Hide, who accord-ingly migrated southeast to *Me'etsendāne* Lake. By 1930, eight families lived at this location (Canada, Dept. Indian Affairs, 1930). *Me'etsendāne* villagers came in contact with non-Natives when they travelled to fur-trade posts where mercantile, religious, and government agents resided (Sheppard 1983b, 339–40). In 1933, Catholic missionaries began regular visits to *Me'etsendāne* via dogsled or float plane, and in 1938, the priests built a church there (Carpentier 1938–46).

Life at Caribou Hide and *Me'etsendāne* revolved around trapping and sustenance hunting and, occasionally, guiding foreign hunters in search of trophy game. Hunters sustained themselves with *hodzih*, 'caribou'; *kedā*, 'moose'; and smaller game animals such as *didiye*, 'groundhogs' (marmots). Trapping supplemented these activities; a large-scale fur trade, says Sheppard, was already declining (1983b, 335–36), and earnings from trapping paid for manufactured goods and dried, non-perishable foods (345).

Today, elders share vivid memories of life at *Me'etsendāne*. They describe trapping expeditions that included men, women, and children. Iskut women also talk about remaining with their youngsters while men travelled to local forts to trade furs. The women add that they hunted moose to feed their families. Travelling long distances is a constant theme in these stories. Likewise, many accounts refer to small cash incomes, good food, and fancy clothes. This talk refutes the notions of hardship and starvation that Walker claimed to have found when he arrived in 1948 (Walker 1976; Henderson 2006). Some elders admit that finding food within easy walking distance became more difficult but add that their survival was never in question.

Residents abandoned *Me'etsendāne* in 1948, perhaps because of illness. Flu struck the Iskut people in 1948 or early 1949 and was probably a cause of one death (Walker to Indian Superintendent Sampson, 15 March 1949, in Walker, various dates; 1976, 160). A decline in the numbers of game animals and the lure of services at *Tlēgōhīn* may also have spurred the exodus from the Spatsizi Plateau. At first, the families moved to semi-permanent camps along the trail on the way to *Tlēgōhīn*. Some moved eastward to forts Grahame and Ware in the Finlay valley. In 1948–49, many wintered at the confluence of the Ross and Stikine rivers (Indian Superintendent Sampson to Walker, 9 April 1949, in Walker, various dates). Two Iskut families arrived at Walker's camp at *Hok'ats Łuwe Menh* on 1 October 1950 and stayed there for the winter. Some families moved all the way to *Tlēgōhīn* in 1948, and others followed by 1951 (Walker 1976, 185).

The Indian agent and the priests at *Tlēgōhīn* pressed Iskut families to settle in *Tlēgōhīn* (Walker to Federal Indian Commissioner, 10 October 1950, in Walker, various dates), which now had stores, services, and schools. Other Iskut ancestors were already living closer to *Tlēgōhīn* at points along the main trail. A mission and school had gone up at *Łuwechōn Menh* in 1936, and some Iskut families were spending the spring and summer there (Carpentier 1938–46). Still other Iskut families had established a village at Buckley Lake,[17] on the trail between *Tlēgōhīn* and *Łuwechōn Menh*, and the priests from *Tlēgōhīn* had begun to serve it too. By 1952, the federal Department of Indian Affairs created a new permanent village site – the Commonage – for *Me'etsendāne* families opposite *Tlēgōhīn*, on the south side of the Stikine River. Thus, after 1948, families that now call Iskut Village home lived in various camps between *Tlēgōhīn* and *Me'etsendāne*. This diaspora contributes to the variations in Iskut history that one hears in the village today.

Discussing these movements in Iskut can elicit bad feelings. Many of the problems stem from the book that Tommy Walker wrote about his life and guiding business on the Spatsizi Plateau (Sheppard 1983b, 14–15). Walker generated considerable resentment when he suggested that the *Me'etsendāne* families were struggling to survive when he arrived in 1948 (Walker 1976). Without the food and employment in the guiding industry that he provided, he implies, the families would have starved (164–67). Iskut people bristle at any suggestion that Walker was responsible for their survival. To them, it was he who needed their help to keep his business running. Many Iskut people became even angrier when it became apparent that Walker helped facilitate relocation to *Tlēgōhīn* – perhaps, some believe, to keep the game for himself (Henderson 2006; Pynn 2006).

The Commonage at Tlēgōhīn *(1950s)*

Tlēgōhīn is also known as Telegraph Creek. It takes its Tahltan name from the Tlingit language (Carter, Carlick, and Carlick 1994, 126) and its English name from its prominent location along a proposed telegraph line from San Francisco to Siberia. Initial plans date back to the 1860s, but that line never started. Although interest in telegraph lines through the settlement resurfaced later in the century (Sheppard 1983b; Neering 1989), *Tlēgōhīn* remained quite isolated from the rest of Canada, even in the 1950s. Visitors to the area arrived via steamer from Wrangell, Alaska. The only alternative approaches were on overland trails or a barge along the Dease River south from the Alaska Highway to the settlement at the head of *Tatl'ah*, whence a rough wagon and truck road of 100 km (60 miles) led to *Tlēgōhīn*.[18]

Many of today's older Iskut adults were born at *Tlēgōhīn* on lands that the federal Department of Indian Affairs had set aside for their families, but the Iskut Commonage never constituted an official reserve.[19] It was on the south side of the lower Stikine River, across from the non-Native and Tahltan villages at *Tlēgōhīn*. The Stikine physically and symbolically separated it from other Tahltan speakers. Elders say that hunting remained a significant sustenance activity during the 1950s. The Commonage served as a base for hunting trips eastward, and, because of the old trail networks, hunting continued in customary family hunting and trapping areas. Notable hunting camps included Buckley Lake (a day's walk to the east), *Łuwechōn* (three to four days' walk to the east), and even one at *Hok'ats Łuwe Menh* on the Spatsizi Plateau (a walk of a week to the east).

Some Commonage families wintered in tents elsewhere during this period. They spent the winter of 1952–53 at *Łuwechōn* and the following winter at Buckley Lake. Several families were at *Tlēgōhīn* during the winters of 1954–55 and 1955–56 (MacLachlan 1956, 18), and others wintered throughout the 1950s at *Łuwechōn, Hok'ats Łuwe Menh*, or Hyland Post on the Spatsizi Plateau (44–45). Elders indicate that during the winter people preferred the familiarity of inland camps and hunting to the Stikine valley. In turn, they appreciated the riverine settlement at the Commonage during salmon fishing in June and July. Iskut elders also describe the importance of sharing moose meat that hunters brought into the Commonage because there were no freezers in which to preserve the meat for long periods.

A home on the Stikine River, below the natural blockages of the Stikine Canyon, provided Iskut families with direct access to the massive Stikine salmon runs for the first time. Prior to this, Iskut people acquired salmon through trade with Tahltan relatives who lived along the Stikine and Tahltan rivers. Iskut families embraced this new sustenance opportunity, building smokehouses and establishing netbooming stations along their side of the river. While few houses from the 1950s remain on the site, people still use these campsites and one smokehouse regularly during June and July. Several Iskut families who lack marriage ties to the *Tlēgōhīn* Tahltans, and thus access to private salmon-fishing sites, continue to camp at the Commonage each July and catch their own sockeye salmon. For Iskut families, owning a land base on the salmon-bearing part of the Stikine is a continuing source of pride.

Tommy Walker's guide-outfitting business at *Hok'ats Łuwe Menh* began to meet with success during the 1950s, too. Iskut men such as Robert Quock and Scotty Edwards (Chapter 4) were regular guides and employees, returning each summer to help him show mostly American hunters the best places to shoot big-horned sheep. Others, such as Alec Jack,[20] stayed through the winter to watch the horses (Walker, various dates). Working for Walker provided Iskut men and women with extended and extensive interactions with business people and wealthy tourists who could afford the long trip to the hunting grounds. The stories of this era endure today, often as commentaries on the good and the bad of life in the past. Peter Rivers recalls with fondness guiding a military fighter pilot. The recollections of other guides include references to the wastefulness of non-Native hunters who wanted to shoot several animals at once. Still other accounts demonstrate both a disdain for Walker's meddling in land management and an appreciation for the work that his outfit provided. This talk is another reminder that Iskut people saw themselves in control of the land and its resources during this era.

Iskut Village (1960s–Present)

Some of today's Iskut families lived at the Iskut site near *Łuwechōn Menh* before 1962, when the Commonage families moved there. Members of these families complain today that the 'official' or band office (and Department of Indian Affairs) history of the village often ignores this earlier habitation. During the 1930s, three extended families camped regularly at the place. Robert Quock, remembering those days, describes hauling water from *Setū* to his family's tent near where the Iskut medical clinic is today. The Catholic missionaries acknowledged the regular encampment and established a school and church near *Łuwechōn Menh* in the 1930s. During the 1940s and 1950s, eleven families with perhaps one hundred people lived at *Łuwechōn Menh* while other Iskut families were building homes near *Tlēgōhīn* (personal communication, Father J.M. Mouchet, 25 July 2004; Arthur Nole, 14 August 2004). These families claim *Łuwechōn* as home before the regional consolidation after 1962 when Iskut Village took its current shape. They never stopped living there and assert as much.

The Commonage families moved to Iskut in 1962 because of tensions between Iskut families and Tahltans at *Tlēgōhīn* (Sheppard 1983b, 344; Walker, various dates). People mentioned this to me, though never in precise terms. Iskut people say that they never truly felt welcome at *Tlēgōhīn* because they were newcomers and because the Stikine separated them from other Tahltan speakers (also Walker 1976, 240). Some describe the move to Iskut as a chance to re-establish independence in a more familiar place. Fur prices were increasing in the early 1960s, and some people wanted to live closer to Iskut traplines. The jobs and services that a move to *Tlēgōhīn* seemed to promise never materialized in a satisfactory way. The building of the highway moved those benefits to the headwaters of the Iskut River.

In a letter addressed to both the minister of Indian Affairs and the minister of Northern Affairs in 1964, the Iskut council sought official status as an Indian band. The councilors rationalized the move from *Tlēgōhīn*: 'We moved to the Iskut Lake village to bring better things for our children, to give them a chance in life . . . We didn't move to

be enemies, we moved so we would have a healthier and better life'
(Walker, various dates, 22 June 1964). The letter emphasizes the benefits of the move while hinting at the tensions that families would leave
behind.

Iskut men and women continued to work for outfitting operations
in the 1960s – for Steele Hyland, who had his base at *Kenes'kani Menh*,
and Walker out of *Hok'ats Łuwe Menh*. By the 1970s, that generation of
outfitters retired, and the Collingwood Brothers of Smithers, British
Columbia, became the big players on the Spatsizi. In the 1980s, the
Iskut First Nation established its own outfitting operation, which continues to attract hunters today. Major infrastructure changes came in
the 1960s and 1970s, too. The Stewart-Cassiar Highway completed a
link between central British Columbia and the Alaska Highway, and
regular shipments of freight followed; tourists arrived too. BC Rail's
attempt to build a line to *Tatl'ah* in the early 1970s failed. Both construction projects triggered changes to hunting practices. Motorized
travel replaced foot travel and use of dogs and sleds, for example.
The unfinished railway bed remains a primary access road for pickup
trucks taking families to weekend and summertime hunting areas
and camps.

It is tempting to attribute changes to the amount of time people
spend hunting today to the advent of the automobile. Elder and former
band chief Louis Louie says that people hunt close to roads today, and
so children 'have it easy' vis-à-vis hunting (Louis Louie, personal communication, 10 February 2003). Some elders assert that youngsters are
not learning about hunting now. They explain this change variously
in terms of lack of interest, a preference for driving snowmobiles and
ATVs recreationally instead of hunting with them, and other activities,
including watching television. But young adults complained to me
that their parents and grandparents were not teaching them the proper
ways to hunt and fish. My observations indicate that ATVs and snowmobiles are indispensable tools for hunting. Hunting is rarely far from
the minds of younger people even when they use these machines recreationally. What constitutes 'being *didene*' depends, in some instances,
on your age.

The Region

Tatl'ah, or Dease Lake, has been a regional centre for commerce since
the second half of the nineteenth century. The Hudson's Bay post there

served the area between 1898 and 1901. In 1837 and 1838, Robert Campbell tried unsuccessfully to establish a post for the company. Suspicion about his motives discouraged Tahltans from the lower Stikine River (at Tahltan River near the present-day site of *Tlēgōhīn*) from supporting his efforts. Some Tahltans say that their ancestors forced him to leave perhaps because of the threat the company posed to trade between Tahltans and Tlingits. There is some evidence that Campbell and his men nearly starved in the winter of 1839 (Sheppard 1983b, 131–40).

Today, *Tatl'ah* remains the bureaucratic and economic centre for northwestern British Columbia. Iskut people have relatives there. They use the government agent's offices to do their banking or renew their driver's licences. And *Tatl'ah* has a sizeable grocery store, by northern standards, and a small liquor outlet. Yet it is not on historical Iskut travel and hunting routes and holds little attraction.

Iskut shoppers visit Terrace or Prince George, British Columbia, a couple of times a year and sometimes more frequently. These towns are seven and ten hours away by car, respectively. They are university and college towns, each with a Wal-mart, Home Depot, and shopping centres. Iskut people have relatives in these places too. Martha James jokes that the Skeena Mall in Terrace is 'Little Iskut' because she always sees people she knows there. For substantial medical needs, including childbirth, Iskut people venture south to hospitals in Terrace or Prince George.

Provincial politics is a preoccupation for many Iskut residents. One issue of particular interest is alienation from parklands. Much of the Spatsizi Plateau area, homeland to so many Iskut families, is now part of a provincial wilderness area that BC Parks manages. Tommy Walker lobbied the BC government to create the Spatsizi Plateau Wilderness Park – his legacy in the province's north (Careless 1997; Henderson 2006; Loo 2006, 193–201). Official designation ended construction of roads and other development in the area but not hunting, and Iskut guides continue to lead non-Native hunters into the area.[21]

Many Iskut people do not like the park status. It has increased government management and bureaucracy in what they claim as their traditional lands. The Iskut leadership is working closely with BC Parks to manage those lands in ways compatible with hunting. Still, Iskut people perceive of the park as an example of meddling by outsiders, and certainly parks are symbolic of the challenges the wider world poses for Iskut people.

Decisions about joining the British Columbia treaty process, and peripheral negotiations with resource companies over mineral and timber rights, have also dominated local politics. In Iskut, the question remains whether or not to negotiate development contracts in association with the Tahltans at *Tlēgōhīn* and *Tatl'ah* or to act independently. The former option – joining with others under the umbrella of a tribal council – has had varying success. Resource and treaty negotiations, however, often work better when greater numbers of people, with a demonstrably large land base, make the claims. The latter option – acting independently – always sounds good but often fails. Different opinions within Iskut Village complicate local and regional politics.

Since 2005, Iskut people and their Tahltan-speaking relatives at *Tlēgōhīn* have participated in a number of civil actions in defence of local management of land and resources. Tahltan elders at *Tlēgōhīn* occupied the First Nation offices in that community for several months early in 2005 to protest the economic and political leadership of the elected chief (Paulson 2006). In the summer and autumn of 2005, Iskut people, mainly women, blocked the road to the BC Rail grade and the Iskut hunting camps to traffic from a mining company trying to explore for coal and methane gas (Carmichael 2005). Protests at Iskut against resource companies continued during the summers of 2006, 2007, and 2008. The civil disobedience caught the attention of Iskut's Athapaskan neighbours to the south, the Wet'suwet'en. Environmental organizations, such as the Skeena Watershed Conservation Coalition of Hazelton, also became active. The Wet'suwet'en and the coalition brought concern for salmon downstream from Tahltan territory into the environmental conflict. The lack of local control over resource development and, indeed, over the actions of band councils has prompted these actions (also Morgan 2009; cf. Feit 2004). Unlike big-game guiding and commercial trapping, which Iskut people embraced as hunting experts, mineral exploration and drilling for gas has been overseen and conducted for decades without significant consultation with Iskut people (e.g., Kerr 1929; Polster and Pituley 1994; Morgan 2009).[22]

Collisions between tradition and modernization have characterized the past century in northwestern British Columbia. Just ask Martha James, who never wants to walk the trails between camps and village sites again; driving between camps is just fine, she comments, because it is easier and more comfortable. The history of the moves around northern BC detailed in this chapter is evidence of both outsiders' intrusions into the region and Iskut adaptation, or not, to those arrivals. Likewise, provincial politics offers an intriguing backdrop for considering the advantages and disadvantages of talking about hunting. The shared history, with variations for each family, is part of the larger hunting legacy stemming from life in British Columbia's north. It provides families with a collective experience on which to base a common identity and culture. It offers points for contentious debates as well. Stories of the hunt (chapter 3), of work with Walker (chapter 4), and of regional politics (chapter 5) illustrate how the mercantile past, which Iskut people participated in so willingly and competently, became a resource-driven present with control over lands and resources located elsewhere, in centres of political power like Victoria or commercial power like Vancouver. Armed with the stories of this history, Iskut people ponder the past and reshape it in novel ways.

PART II

Stories about Hunting and History

3 'That Bloody Moose Got Up and Took Off': Food Animals and Traditional Knowledge[1]

Introduction

I learned from several people in Iskut Village that Arthur Nole was very knowledgeable about fishing and hunting. His knowledge stemmed from the fact that he hunted regularly and had been doing so since he was a boy. But despite my attempts to convince him to invite me along on his hunting expeditions or fishing trips and his general agreement to my participation, I found myself hearing after the fact that he had been out hunting or camping. Then I learned that he was 'moving up' to his *Didini Kime*[2] (camp) for three or four weeks in August (Figure 5). As it turned out, I bumped into him on the BC Rail grade early in August; he was hauling wood to the camp with his grandsons. I stopped him in his truck and asked if I could camp with him later that week. He agreed.

I drove up the BC Rail grade to Arthur's camp a few days later. *Didini Kime* is high in the headwaters of the *Tl'abāne Tū'e* and sits on the eastern flank of *Dẓełtsedle*. My trip from Iskut Village took about four hours, partly because of my cautious driving on the rough and sometimes-flooded gravel roadway. When I pulled into the campsite, Arthur was sitting under the kitchen tarp on a homemade log stool. He was with four of his grandsons, who seemed to know who I was even though I had not met any of them. I asked Arthur again if I could stay. He invited me to put my tent up just outside the main kitchen and living area of the camp. My little green nylon tent seemed feeble next to the robust canvas tents and wooden frames of the camp. I then put my food into the communal pantry boxes and the generator-powered deep-freeze.

Much of my time camping with Arthur involved mundane activities such as cooking, collecting firewood, and hauling water – I was happy

Didini Kime, 'Young Caribou Camp,' is notable for its substantial main camp made of tarpaulins stretched over wood frames, various wood-burning stoves, and a small cabin. Other tent sites are located behind the tent frame pictured here.

to help. I also joined him and his grandsons driving up and down remote sections of the BC Rail grade at dusk, looking for caribou and moose. We spotted grouse and groundhogs frequently. With each animal sighting, Arthur slowed his extended-cab pickup truck, and his grandsons reached for their rifles. Each time, the animals scurried away before the boys could alight from the truck. Those drives were a privilege for me, as I contributed only to a shortage of space in the truck.

A few days after my arrival, Arthur's first cousin Colin Duncan showed up with two grandsons, teenagers from Terrace, British Columbia. They pitched tourist-style, self-standing tents like mine near the centre of Arthur's camp. Arthur and his cousin belong to families that sometimes assert ancestral ties to Gitksan-speaking peoples to the south of Iskut territory. They have spent their lives in and around Iskut and *Tlēgōhīn*, hunting on the Spatsizi Plateau.

Once Arthur and Colin were together, conversations within the camp changed. Stories about hunting, past and present, became more frequent. They sounded like memories of the good days, which the two men shared easily, having spent a lifetime hunting together. But after a couple of days, I began to realize that this was not simply small talk; the tone seemed serious, and the tellings sounded intentional. I wanted to hear more.

Pursuit Stories

Accounts about pursuing moose are common in Iskut hunting talk. They are memories of amazing events in the careers of hunters. They contain traditional expressions of respect for animals and deference to them, and because of their older temporal frame, they contrast with the memories of more recent activities like guiding presented in chapters 4 and 5. The humour characteristic of Iskut people is apparent in the stories. Pursuit stories exemplify the way in which hunters tell each other of their own hunting experience and skill while indirectly valorizing the moose. They illustrate themes in Iskut culture such as social relationships between people and animals: the idea that animals and people exist in a sentient ecology in which powerful animals control the outcome of hunts (cf. Anderson 2002, 116).[3] These stories reveal how hunters organize and comment on social relations within their own families. They indicate, for example, that Iskut people should share food with each other.

Here, I present four animal-pursuit stories about moose. They occurred in rapid succession within a larger conversation between first cousins Arthur Nole and Colin Duncan. The two relatives are in their sixties. They have spent their lives in and around Iskut Village and *Tlēgōhīn*. They have hunted on the Spatsizi Plateau and in the *Hok'āz Tū'e* watershed in the *Tl'abāne*. Arthur's hunting punctuates a busy life of caring for grandchildren and working full-time in the village. The region around Iskut has many cabins and camps that he built and maintains – physical evidence of his hunting prowess and his commitment to gathering food for himself, his family, and his community. Colin lives in Terrace but spent many years in Iskut.

As I noted above, these stories sound like small talk. Coupland (2003) says that speakers use small talk to build rapport or credibility, but in this case rapport already existed. I consider these stories a form of small talk that I call 'serious chatter,' or chatter with serious intent. Serious chatter is like 'idle chatter' or 'shooting the breeze' in that it functions mostly to pass the time (see Mears 2002). But when conversation contains allusions to myth-time and uses humour to call attention to it, such dialogue carries more weight than other forms of small talk. In the stories that I examine in this chapter, the serious chatter revolves around hunters discussing hunting and reinforcing bonds of friendship and family. It differs from, for example, Frankfurt's 'bullshitting' (Frankfurt 1986; also cited in Mears 2002) or Goffman's 'fabrication' (Goffman 1986, 83), where the teller intends to deceive. These tales of pursuing moose include temporary deception only, as each implies that the hunter has killed the animal before revealing that it had escaped. And this deception points to my interest in these stories: the Tahltan values that they convey.[4]

The more I listened to Arthur's and Colin's hunting stories, the more central to camp life they seemed to be. The boys in the camp could not help but hear the stories too. The accounts were thin on details, however. They sounded plausible, but when did they occur? Who was there? I started to wonder if the teller intended to deflect attention away from the violence of hunting. The stories sounded consistent with the observations of Subarctic anthropologists that hunters must kill the animals they also revere (e.g., Tanner 1979; Brightman 1993; Preston 2002; Nadasdy 2005). How did talk about killing moose show respect to the animals? And what about the observation that these stories were replete with details of hunting prowess?

It was at Arthur's camp that I realized that other Iskut women and men had been sharing stories like these for months. I had not, however, been enough in tune with the banter to know that something important was happening. I had been looking for the 'rules' of fishing and the 'gems' of hunting knowledge – those tidbits that could fit easily in the column for TEK (traditional ecological knowledge) in a database. The intensity with which Arthur and Colin spoke about hunting told me that I had been missing the heart of the verbal action. I sensed that the speakers were debating hunting practices and history, and I became desperate to record their stories.

Transcript 3.1: Moose Hunting Stories

These accounts of chasing moose form a subset of the hunting talk heard in Arthur Nole's hunting camp. I used a tape recorder to capture all conversations between Arthur and Colin over the course of an hour. For most of that time, the two men sat under Arthur's kitchen tarp near the camp's central cooking fire. The stories are short – no longer than a minute – and each emerges in brief conversational turns in English.[5] They describe the failure of Arthur or Colin to kill a moose that he sees while travelling in the bush near Iskut.

The men spoke in English, and while my presence may have affected the tone or content of the talk, it is unlikely that they would have deviated from their habitual use of English and spoken in Tahltan if I had not been present. Arthur was aware that I wanted to record stories of the old days. For this reason, I may have been a catalyst for these discussions in much the way Oblate priest Father Mouchet described himself as a sounding board for discussions of hunting and history while travelling the trails with Iskut men in the 1950s (Mouchet 2002, 55). Still, I did not ask for the men to give these accounts. And the large number of stories I heard in this setting and in others suggests to me that the cousins would have shared these accounts whether I was there or not.

I divide the transcript into six segments. The first segment (A) consists of the conversation leading up to the stories. It provides readers with a sense of the abrupt beginning to the exchange between Arthur and Colin. The next segments (B–E) are the four stories. Colin initiates the exchanges in segment B, and the storytellers alternate turns thereafter. Segment F is the last stretch of talk. Bobby Weeks, one of Arthur's grandsons, inserts himself into the exchange to ask if he can go hunting. There are no significant pauses between stories. I have not eliminated any dialogue from the transcript.[6]

Speakers:
AN – Arthur Nole (61 years old)
CD – Colin Duncan (60–65)
BW – Bobby Weeks (15)
JW – James William (15)

[Setting: Arthur and Colin are sitting under a kitchen tarp in a hunting camp. Colin sits at the kitchen table and Arthur on a stool about three feet away. I am sitting next to the fire, three feet from both men. Two teenaged boys move in and out of the setting as they prepare their gear for hunting *dediye*, 'groundhogs.'[7]]

A. Lead-in (lines 1–15)

1   CD   Who's got his [Arthur's father] gun?   [0:00]

     AN   I got it at home.

CD   Oh.

BW   What kind?

5   CD   .303.

AN   Frank[8] wanted it,
            but he told me to keep his gun.
                'I just wanna raise you kids,'
            he say.

10   BW   .303?

AN   Yeah.

CD   Good shootin' gun.

AN   I shot quite a bit moose with it.
            'You keep it
15   so you kill moose with it.'   [0:24.54]

B. Colin Duncan story no. 1 (lines 16–51)

CD   We travel here.   [0:25.48]
        Go get that moose.
        'Way I go.
        Too much,
20   I wanna make one shot with it,
        his gun.
        His gun is so good.
        One time I got burnt there, eh.
        Come along to that moose and
25   'boom.'
        Here I musta shoot through the [*pause*] weather bone, eh.
                                                    [*laughs*]

AN   weather bone.
                                                    [*laughs*][9]

CD   I snowshoe around him.

And we keep agoin'.
30 And I think I'll get it up on top
and it'll come.
Big valley on other side
and he'll come on through.
Then I went back,
35 and uncle,
we had camp down below.
He [the uncle] make everybody look.
'Hey Scotty,[10]
look at that.'
40 Here that moose get up and run.
Way he go down the hill.
I didn't know that, you know.
He came out
and look at my moose.
45 It's gone.
I look right out.
It's running away.
[laughter with AN]
Then I coulda shot him again.
50 I just thought,
'ah that's good enough.'   [1:10.55]

C. Arthur Nole story no. 1 (lines 52–83)

AN   That's what I did,   [1:12.20]
son of a gun.
I had 30-30
55 and I shot moose.
'Bikū.'[11] [gestures, see below]
'Bikū.'
Down he went.
He kick around, eh
60 And he quit.
I thought he died.
I made trail back to my dog team.
All the way to the dogs,
back and forth.

65   So I got two.
               That first bull
               I tip it over.
               I started to skin it.
               I finished skinning it
70   I thought
                     'I should get my dogs,
                       go to that cow.'
             No,
             I went over to that cow.
75   Here it ditch up that hill.

CD   [*laughs*]

AN   Gee,
           I run up behind it
           I come out.
80   I see it
           but I miss.

CD   It happened to me twice.   [1:57.26]

AN   Break trail for nothing.   [1:59.57]

D. Colin Duncan story no. 2 (lines 84–99)

CD   Happened to me top of Stikine.   [2:01.55]
85   Wife and I come out around that long stretch.
           See this cow moose run off, eh,
           in the timber.
           He stop.
                    'Bang.'
90   Down he went.
           I went back to the truck.
           Drove my truck up there.
           Got my packboard.
           Put on my snowshoes.
95   Went back there.
           The bloody moose got up
           and took off.

AN   [*laughs*]   [2:19.80]

CD   Twice I got burned like that.   [2:23.80]

E. Arthur Nole story no. 2 (lines 100–34)

100   AN   I did same thing   [2:26.40]
           other end, outlet of *Mo'uchōhe*.[12]
           I shot one dead.
           The other one I shot.
           Big cow too.
105   I shot and he drop.
           I keep it on.
           He quit so far.
           Thought I got two moose.
           I walk over to the first one.
110   He's dead.
           I went over to the other one.
           There he got up.
           I look.
           Here he's in a poplar. [*with disbelief*]
115   Oh, how I shoot [?].
           I miss it
           and I chase it.
           He fall down three times, eh.
           From there he's gone.
120   I hit him right there with it.
           I went back to skin the other one.
           I was going to make skin toboggan.
           I walk right across the lake.
           My skidoo over there.
125   Bring it,
           go down.
           Whole moose,
           I drag out to the highway.
           I bury it.
130   And I walk down to Monty Able
           where they call Cready Cabin,
           It's about a mile and a half.

He help me out.
He haul that meat for me.   [3:28.00]

F. Conversation after the stories

135   BW   What time, gramps?   [3:31.75]

       AN   Ten to two.

       BW   Think there'd be groundhogs comin' out?

       CD   Comin' out,
                 yeah,
140   if sun come out.
                 They'll come out.

       JW   Okay. Let's go.

       BW   Let's go up.
                 You'll take your.22 then.   [3:47.00]

                                            (13 August 2002)

The Structure of Pursuit Stories

In most of the dialogue here, the speaker overtly addresses the other
person. There is almost no reported speech. The action revolves around
the interaction of narrator and moose. Colin interacts with one moose
in each of his stories; Arthur kills one moose and misses another in
his. What is noteworthy is the careful structure. Each story contains
seven units and revolves around a narrative turn in which the teller
announces that the hunted moose has escaped or that the shot missed
the target.

The seven units are as follows:
    I. introductory frame
    II. set-up for the rifle shot
    III. the shot
    IV. result of the shot
    V. activity after the shot

VI. the narrative turn
VII. ending: giving up and moving on

Colin Duncan starts off (unit I; line 16). He departs from the preceding conversation about a family rifle. The rifle motivates the story, albeit indirectly; not surprisingly, rifles and their use are common features of hunting talk. Arthur takes his turn quickly after Colin finishes his first narrative. Arthur states: 'That's what I did / son of a gun' (lines 52–53). Colin takes the turn back with 'Happened to me top of Stikine' (line 84). Arthur's second story starts, 'I did same thing' (line 100).

After the conversational turn, each man offers basic information about the moose and minor details about the broader context of the hunt (unit II). This information includes the type of rifle, the first appearance of the moose, its sex, or where the narrator was when he spotted the moose. At the start of his second story, Colin says: 'Wife and I come around that long stretch. / See this cow moose run off, eh, / in the timber. / He's gone' (lines 85–88). In both of his accounts, Arthur mixes the descriptions of killing one moose and missing another. In the first (segment C), he says that he shot two moose (line 65), although Colin and I soon learn that only one moose is dead. In his second (segment E), Arthur also complicates the setup by saying that he shot two moose. He starts by setting one scene: 'other end, outlet of Mo'uchōhe [Lake]' (line 101). After a pause, he continues, telling us that he killed one moose and wounded a cow (lines 102–4).

The two cousins have only described the hunt at this point. Both men establish the claims of personal experience in the opening lines of each story. They authenticate their own authority with references to personal experience and a rifle. They confirm the veracity of the account prior to a dramatic climax – the rifle shot – and an eventual fall in dramatic progression with the unanticipated flight of the moose. The stories are serious in tone. The tellers suggest only that they are describing a successful hunt. There is no laughter. By leading the other teller to assume that he has killed a moose, each narrator leaves open the possibility of an unexpected turn later in the narrative.

A rifle shot is a central feature of each story (unit III). The teller identifies the shot audibly and, in one case, visually with hand gestures. Colin uses the words 'boom' (line 25) in his first account and 'bang' (line 89) in his second. Arthur is somewhat more dramatic in his first story, repeating the onomatopoeic word 'bikū' (lines 56–57). He accompanies the word with a shooting gesture, holding both arms loosely in the position a shooter holds a rifle. Arthur bends his right arm and holds his right hand near his cheek. He extends his left arm, with a slight bend in the elbow. He turns his head so that he can look down the length of his extended left arm as if he were looking down the barrel of a rifle. From this position, he brings together the fingers and thumbs on both hands, opening the fingers abruptly in the instant that he says 'bikū.' He reports his second shot less dramatically: 'I shot, and he drop' (line 105). Honigmann notes that Kaska hunters telling stories use a similar gesture to aid communication (1949, 138–39).

Arthur jumbles the basic sequence of events in both stories by reporting both successful and unsuccessful kills. In segment C, he uses two expressions to signal early on that he killed only one of the moose. For the successful attempt, he combines the reference to the shot with a definitive statement of the result: 'I shot one dead' (line 102). He continues, describing the second shot in terms that make it sound successful, but without using the word 'dead.' He says simply, 'The other one I shot' (line 103). In segment E, something similar happens to him. Here we learn that the first moose is dead (line 110) but that when Arthur went over to check the second animal it had stood up and left (lines 112–14).

The narrator always announces the result of the shot immediately after the shot sounds (unit IV). In segment C, Arthur says simply, 'Down he went' (line 58). Here he uses a second gesture, dropping his forearm, to represent the animal's fall as he says this line. In segment D, Colin tells Arthur and me the same thing: 'Down he went' (line 90). And in segment E, Arthur is equally straightforward: 'I shot, and he drop' (line 105).

The result of Colin's first shot (segment B) is somewhat more complicated. Colin states: 'Here I musta shoot through the weather bone' (line 26). Both hunters complete the sentence, saying 'weather bone' together, and laughter results (line 27). A shot through the weather bone is not always deadly to a moose, and Arthur's ability to complete Colin's sentence may imply that this has happened to him in the past. Arthur's laughter contributes to this impression and suggests that he has interpreted Colin's description of the wounded animal as the climax or narrative turn of the story. Colin in fact maintains control of the conversational turn and heightens anticipation and suspense further to reveal a more substantial unexpected moment later in the story.

After shooting at the moose, both hunters describe the activities that lead to the revelation that the moose survived (unit V). In the narration, these activities include speculating that the moose is dead and preparing to retrieve it. The descriptions build suspense and delay the climax by creating narrative distance between the shot and the revelation that the moose has survived. Arthur says: 'I thought he died. / Made trail back to my dog team. / All the way to the dogs, / back and forth' (lines 61–64). Later he reports: 'Thought I got two moose . . . I went over to the other one. / There he got up' (lines 108–12). In his first story, Colin has already hinted that he had not killed the animal (line 26). Still he develops his story by describing his efforts to track the fleeing beast. He mentions snowshoeing after the moose and then adds a side sequence (Goffman 1981, 7) about returning to camp and telling his cousin and uncle about the animal (lines 34–40). In his second story, he delays his announcement of the escaping moose by describing his return to his truck to get his packboard and snowshoes (lines 91–95). These extra details delay the expected climax and maintain the possibility that Colin's hunt is ultimately successful.

The actual results of the hunts emerge just before the end of each story (unit VI). In each case, the moose has escaped and the narrators remain behind. Laughter follows in three cases (lines 48, 76, and 99). At the turning point in Arthur's second account, however, there is no laughter, and instead Arthur reveals the failure through intonation signalling disbelief: 'Oh, how I shoot [?]' (line 115). There is no rising intonation at the end of this sentence, but the effect is one of questioning audibly his misfire and disbelieving that the moose is alive and standing in a grove of poplar trees (line 114). Arthur's self-deprecating presentation increases the dramatic fall of the storyline and identifies his missed shot as a spectacular failure; perhaps the great drama that Arthur tells in this last tale signals to Colin that the story exchange does not need to continue.

At best, the amusing moments in these stories are indeed funny to the audience; they may, however, reflect more accurately the level to which the narrator feels uncomfortable revealing their failure to kill the moose. Notably, the grandchildren sitting within earshot did not react to the accounts at all, preferring, in my estimation, to tolerate the chatter of their grandfathers.

The moose got the better of the hunter on these days (unit VII). For Arthur, the attempt at a kill had been a waste of time. It is as if the moose was never going to be killed. In his first story, the disgust is audible: Arthur describes running behind the fleeing animal and ultimately deciding that he had broken trail 'for nothing' (83). In his second tale, he reports again that he ran after the moose in the poplar trees but that, despite its wounds, it escaped (lines 117–20). Colin, too, accepts the failure of the hunt. In his first story he says, 'I coulda shot him again. / I just thought, / ah, that's good enough' (lines 49–51). At the end of his second, he seems to feel both annoyed and amused by his failure: 'Twice I got burned like that' (line 99). These final sequences in all stories provide a denouement as well as a cue to the other person that the narrative has ended.

Bobby's interrupting his grandfather to ask the time breaks the storytelling frame in line 135. A broader discussion ensues around the kitchen table about whether or not it is a good time of day to hunt groundhogs. Bobby was not continuously present in the kitchen during the narration of the four stories. He had just returned, anxious to ask his question between tales. It is possible, however, that he knew that the story was over and that he could take the speaking turn without interrupting his grandfather. Almost four full seconds elapsed between Arthur's last words and Bobby's interruption – a longer pause than that between any of the other stories. This suggests that Colin was not anxious to seize the turn back from Arthur and had perhaps run out of corresponding narratives to share. The extended pause also opened up the conversation to other participants.

Creating Distance from Animals by Indirection and Allusion

Most Iskut residents know the structure of animal-pursuit stories, which suggests that they hear such accounts frequently (Valentine 1995:168). I heard a seven-year-old child use this structure to tell about shooting a *dih*, 'chicken' (grouse). In that case, the boy's shot was successful. There was no 'failure to reveal,' so units VI and VII were missing (McIlwraith 2007, 111–12). Moreover, the structure of pursuit stories permits commentary about the treatment of animals to accompany general talk of the hunt. They draw on elements of Tahltan mythology, including requirements that hunters act properly towards the animals.[13]

Teit's recording of the Tahltan myth-time story 'Meat-Mother and the Caribou and Moose' lays out this rule clearly. 'The Meat-Mother watches her children, the game, and also the people. When people do not follow the taboos, and do not treat animals rightly, the latter tell their mother; and she punishes the people by taking the game away for a while, or by making it wild, and then the people starve ... The Moose children are the most apt to tell their mother of any disrespect shown them: therefore people have to be very careful as to how they treat moose' (Teit 1919, 231–32). Arthur's and Colin's stories are myth-like and, like _sa'e_ stories, contain serious themes about proper treatment of animals and present them within an obvious and regular structure.

Moreover, the hunting stories are commentaries on the continuing importance of social relationships between humans and animals (Ingold 2000; Blaser et al. 2010). Because they appear to be about only spectacular failures, they seem to be indirect commentaries on hunting success and its role in family sustenance. They tell why failed shots are both intensely disappointing and incidental in a hunter's long career. They show that life goes on after failures and that it is easy to laugh at one's mistakes. They index the sacrifice of food animals – the control these animals have over their own life and death – by pointing to powerful moose that decide the outcome of hunts (see Brightman 1993; cf. Hubert and Mauss 1964 [1898]). Notably, the moose in these tales do not give themselves up to the hunter. The sacrificial exchanges are underway as the narration progresses, but in each case the animal decides to leave. What did Arthur or Colin do to discourage each moose from giving itself up? Were they disrespectful in some way? Did they speak badly about moose? Sometimes moose simply escape unexpectedly (Feit 2004, 104). The answers are not forthcoming.[14]

The stories give Arthur and Colin a chance to discuss respectfully, albeit covertly, the ability of moose to stymie a hunting event. The men use a humorous narrative turn to reveal their own inferiority and, indirectly, to describe their frustrations about a moose's behaviour. The use of humour to deflect criticism and to level social differences is visible in many situations at Iskut. Teasing and joking behaviour mark, for example, sibling and cousin relationships during competitive card playing or stick gambling. Card players tease each other over misplays, poor shuffling, and feigned attempts at cheating. During stick-gambling matches, skilled teams distract opponents using techniques such as loud singing, boisterous dancing, and shaming. To talk about moose directly, or critically, might seem disrespectful and result in punishment by Meat Mother. Moose are, after all, more powerful than hunters. The stories also permit a hunter to discuss at length past hunts that do not show up the other hunters through self-aggrandizement.

A focus on the failure creates rhetorical distance from both the moose and the hunter's own prowess. It masks bravado.

Iskut people often, if unintentionally, assign sentience to moose in less dramatic ways. They say that moose and caribou are aware of the intentions of the people they meet. Moose are, for example, more likely to reveal themselves to people who do not have rifles with them. When spotting a moose, someone inevitably says, 'We saw that because we didn't have a rifle,' or 'We wouldn't have seen that moose if we had a rifle with us.' As in the stories, in these passing remarks a rifle rhetorically mediates relations between hunter and hunted. Moose and caribou know the difference between cameras and rifles. They often posed for my camera, even though my stopping a truck and taking a photograph require a hasty routine and a stance similar to firing a rifle. Moose may know, for that matter, the difference between anthropologists and hunters. It behooves any observer to act carefully and respectfully.

We can extend analysis of hunter-prey relations in stories about moose pursuit, and indeed in general rules for treating food animals, to Iskut social relations. The stretch of speech above begins with Colin Duncan's asking Arthur Nole who now possesses Arthur's father's rifle (line 1). Arthur responds that he has the gun at home (line 2). He adds that his younger brother, Frank, had some interest in keeping the weapon (line 6). He then reports his father's remark that he 'just wanna raise you kids' (line 8) – referring presumably to Frank, Arthur, and their siblings. The father's voice appears to re-enter the conversation soon. Arthur tells Colin that his father wanted him to keep the rifle and to kill a lot of moose with it (lines 14–15). In this short stretch of talk, the two men evoke their parents' generation with reference to a family rifle. The weapon is symbolic of hunting itself, the power to take an animal's life, as Arthur himself observes. Yet around the symbol develop family relations, the lessons that fathers teach sons, and the rivalry of brothers. The stories depart from here.

The narratives continue to revolve around families. Colin's first story includes direct reference to uncles and nephews (lines 35–37). With that short comment, Colin draws a larger family into his otherwise solitary pursuit of the moose. His failure, in fact, becomes evident first to other people in the camp, which implies their interest in his activities. Arthur's stories do not include such material, but they point to another aspect of the session's discussion of social relationships. Arthur and Colin provide an audience for each other, and each of them clearly plays off of the other's stories. As cousins who both lived in Iskut in the 1950s, they neither offer nor expect contextual details.

Likewise, the children in the camp form an indirect audience for them. Just as the conversation develops from connections between a father and his children, the storytelling itself continues a tradition of sharing news and history between generations. The stories signal the instructional and mentoring relationships that older hunters share with younger boys. The immediate importance of hunting returns in the final segment when Bobby Weeks approaches to ask if he and his brother and their cousins can go hunting. A rifle is central to that talk, too. The stories remind listeners, including me, that senior men have obligations to teach hunting practices and how to care for animals. Doing so might be more important than actually killing a moose.

Transcript 3.2: Reporting a Successful Moose Kill

Hunting and speaking about hunting shape connections between people and between people and animals at Iskut Village. But managing those relationships is always a challenge. Contradictions abound. While Arthur and Colin offer a careful exchange that avoids direct boasting about the demise of moose, this is not always the case. The reporting of moose kills can, for example, evoke pride and provoke amusement. In the following conversation (transcript 3.2), two women comment on a successful hunt by the husband of one of them.

[Setting: Janice and Ginny, sisters-in-law, talk about the hunting activities of Janice's husband. The conversation occurs in the lobby of the Iskut First Nation band office.]

1	Janice	Dennis [Janice's husband] got a moose yesterday.
2	Ginny	I heard. He called Gord [Ginny's husband] at lunch.
3	Janice	He was funny about it.
4		He came in and said he got skunked again.
5		Long time since we didn't get one.
6		We been almost out of meat.

(19 January 2003)

The feigned failure might have had serious consequences for Janice's family had it been true; she admits that they have not had fresh meat in quite some time (lines 5–6). Her comment that Dennis acted 'funny' (line 3) reminds me of the enjoyment Iskut people receive when they hold back information or report falsehoods simply to provoke an

emotional response. Notably, Janice did not feel any reluctance in telling this story – and in effect describing a successful hunt – to Ginny.
Presumably, Dennis reported the successful kill as a failure to tease his
wife. Such banter is part of the good-natured relationships between
spouses and between siblings that I witnessed time and again. This
sort of kidding also plays down the success of the hunter and, perhaps,
valorizes the moose. It represents an indirect way of revealing that the
hunter killed the moose. In most cases, boasting about one's accom-
plishments is considered bad form.

More generally, villagers talk about respect for and proper treatment
of animals in straightforward statements while camping or collecting
food. As they do in the moose stories above, they express these statements matter-of-factly and rarely with additional explanation. They
offer them while, for example, teaching children or anthropologists
how to behave in order to secure food. While cutting wood with Peter
Rivers and his grandchildren, one of the teenaged boys told me that
whistling at rabbits makes them stop running from you. On another
occasion, a young man in his early twenties revealed to me that the
elders taught him that you can catch or shoot an animal only when it
agrees to give itself to you. I learned that birds can lead you to a moose.
While sitting on a stool in his camp, Arthur Nole shared a story about a
'camp robber' (the grey jay, *Perisoreus canadensis*) that led him to moose.
He added that he gives camp robbers moose fat in exchange for their
help in finding moose. In all these cases, personal associations or interactions with some animals help with hunting.

Young people, more often than elders, reminded me that once an animal appears in front of a hunter, he or she must take it. I encountered
this rule, and a violation of it, while travelling with Iskut friends near
the village. A moose appeared in front of my truck. After I slowed to
look at it, someone told me to drive on. We had a rifle with us, and I was
uncertain about why no one shot the animal. The rifle owner hinted,
however, that he was unwilling to butcher and clean the moose that
day. It was too much work, he said. I wondered if he was referring to
my presence and the fact that he would have to teach me what to do.
Back in Iskut, Michael Roe,[15] a man in his early forties, chastised the
man emphatically for not shooting the moose. In Tahltan, Michael said
directly to him: *ensuge dintsel* ('You will eat your fart').[16] Without meat,
he implied, we had only our stomach gases to sustain us.

The rules about shooting moose are numerous and complicated.
Hunters are reluctant to shoot them in late winter and spring for fear

of shooting a pregnant cow. Likewise, they say that after the winter, moose are dirty and thin. According to Michael Roe, the choice not to shoot a moose relates to both the quality of the meat and conservation efforts (Michael Roe, personal communication, 4 August 2002). To be worthy of shooting, he says, the meat from the kill must be of high quality. The best meat is on a young bull moose, one that has visibly thicker fat over the shoulders and back. Some hunters choose not to shoot a moose that looks thin or is too old. Similarly, hunters avoid taking bull moose and caribou during the autumn rutting season because they are 'dirty' or 'smelly.' They stay away from cow moose that are potentially bearing young as a way of 'conserving' (Michael's word) the animal for future years.

With these assessments, Michael combines an older practice – evaluation of the quality of the meat – with seeming concern for conserving moose. He talks about conservation in terms that conservation officers would appreciate and understand, especially because status Indians are not subject to British Columbia's hunting regulations (also Nadasdy 2005).

Michael's comments represent one side of the meat-quality debate in Iskut. Ken James, a man in his early thirties, values quality meat but is not so 'picky' as to wait for the ideal moose. He elaborates, turning his thoughts to mountain sheep: 'I'd like to get a nice ram, or at least a decent one.' This suggests a hierarchy of meat animals, and Ken concedes that a decent moose is one with an inch or more of fat on it; he does not say what a nice ram might be (Ken James, personal communication, 23 February 2003). Martha James also offers an alternative view to the notion that meat quality determines a hunter's decision to shoot. She says that when Iskut families were living at older settlements such as Me'etsendāne, Buckley Lake, or Tlēgōhīn, they would take any animal that they saw. The need for food demanded that hunters shoot cows and thin bulls (Martha James, personal communication, 14 January 2004). From Martha's perspective, the decision not to shoot an animal with poor meat is a recent phenomenon and flows perhaps from the availability of contemporary conveniences. Michael, for instance, can choose to shoot or not because he can save the rewards of previous hunts in his freezer or, if need be, visit the store to pick up supplies.

People of all ages know these injunctions and enforce them through direct and indirect discourse or actions. Adult hunters, for example, tell their children directly not to talk badly about animals, tease them, or play with them (also Sheppard 1983b; Nadasdy 2003, 88–91). Children enact these rules explicitly. I watched one evening in August 2004 as Laura and Cliff Rivers butchered a caribou in front of five young teenagers on the slope of *Dzełtsedle*. As Laura began to open the caribou's belly with her knife, one boy exclaimed, 'nasty,' in response to the warm air and smell that came from the body. Immediately and in unison, the other four kids chided their cousin: 'Don't say that. Don't talk bad about it.' This embarrassed the boy. Such direct and indirect criticism of the actions of others keeps the rules in play (Nadasdy 2005, 306–7).

Less direct ways of controlling behaviour include making passing references to being 'stingy.' 'Acting stingy' is a particularly serious label for people who do not share what they have (also Braroe 1975, 150–6; Sheppard 1983b, 538; Smith 2002). To be sure, Arthur and Colin's stories address stinginess only indirectly; the moose in them survive the hunt and thus act in a stingy way. Being stingy violates proper social relations *between people*. The Tahltan word for stingy – *eghādetsen'* – has nothing to do with meat, according to one elder, even though it appears to contain the Tahltan word *etsen'*, 'meat.' *Tsēghādetsen'*, 'Stingy Mountain,' is southeast of *Tlēgōhīn* and visible from the town. The name comes from hunters who report frequent sightings of goats on the mountain, yet other hunters observe none there. In this case, the land itself acts in a stingy way and withholds food from hunters.

In times past, the phrase 'acting stingy' referred to people who did not share food. During shortages, hoarding could put others at risk of starvation. David Smith (2002, 65) notes that among the Chipewyans, humans' stinginess stands in contrast to animals who give themselves up to hunters selflessly. He elaborates, saying that between people 'stinginess can be as reprehensible as murder, and . . . it sometimes was tantamount to murder' (65). Avoiding stinginess suggests that generosity and sharing are better (Sheppard 1983b, 563). Martha James, referring to her granddaughter, who had eaten a half-bag of *etsen' gāne*, 'dry [moose] meat,' said to me: 'How stingy.'

I heard often that the arrival of freezers in the village made people stingy because families could now store meat without sharing it. While their advent has certainly permitted stinginess, a freezer simply allows people to hunt less frequently before food spoils. I suspect that some people hunt more, store more food, and share food widely at community feasts. The freezer has essentially extended winter, or at least the preservation of food that cold weather provides, for people able to continue hunting. Villagers avoid stingy neighbours, just as hunters stay away from stingy land.

Generosity is the opposite of stinginess. Hunters share meat from successful hunts with family members and others. This distribution of food draws non-hunters into hunting activities. Martha James's family is typical. Her grandsons hunt together or with their father, Martha's son-in-law. After a successful moose hunt, they take the meat to her house, where the grandsons hang the meat in her smokehouse or basement. She cuts and salts some of the meat for dry meat jerky. She controls that production, returning some of the meat to her family and keeping the rest for her own use or for sale around the village.

The term 'stingy' has acquired meanings outside of its original contexts of hunting and sharing meat. On a visit to Vancouver, I heard Susan Folke say, 'I act stingy to myself,' in reference to cutting short her own shopping spree. The word also surfaces frequently around the card table. One evening, while playing the card game Thirty-One, Martha James and I sat side by side in an arrangement that required that I pass cards to her. According to the rules of the game, Martha would see a selection of cards I might pass to her, and on several occasions I chose to give her poor cards – I was keeping the good ones for myself. Money was at stake, after all. After one such pass, Martha feigned anger and said, 'You Stingy Mountain,' and then laughed aloud. By invoking this name, she criticized my play. She hoped to influence me the next time I faced a similar choice. It worked.

Peter Rivers spoke frequently about the ability to procure and secure food when the opportunity presents itself. The first time he took me ice fishing at *Łuwechōn Menh*, I failed to catch anything. As we packed up our gear, he turned to me and without a grin said: 'I'm not going to starve in this country, but you will.' I took his comment as a lighthearted tease, but I learned later that older adults often use this refrain to call attention to a child's laziness or ignorance about hunting. It can also be a comment about the ability of a good fisherman to feed himself and the potential to go hungry if he fails.

Then Peter gave me two of the *deghai* ('rainbow trout,' *Oncorhynchus mykiss*) that he had caught. He had not cleaned the fish, and I moved to cut its head off before Peter thought it was dead. He told me, 'You gotta kill it before you gut it, or they'll punish you.' This comment startled me, and I whacked the fish in the back of the head with my knife, as I had seen Peter do. I asked him about the punishment and to whom he was referring. He responded: 'How would you like to be gutted if you were still alive?' He never elaborated on who 'they' were or what the punishment could be.

Iskut people rarely explain such things. By making me feel much like an Iskut child, the message hit me hard enough to make sure that I clubbed any fish I caught in the future hard enough to ensure that it was dead. Now I see Peter's message as implicating me in the web of life within which Iskut people act. I also understand Peter's words as a reminder that once a fish offers itself to you, you must kill it. Otherwise you starve.[17]

Non-Native hunters are not exempt from punishment by animals. Iskut people cite them as examples of what may result when people violate proper relations with animals. Trapper Terry MacMillan (not a pseudonym) froze to death on a back road several hours from Iskut in 1993. Villagers interpret this sad episode as an example of both Terry's poor planning and his mistreatment of a grizzly bear. Terry lived in a trailer at the headwaters of the Skeena River. He was a decent trapper, by all accounts, and Iskut hunters knew him well. But he usually did not prepare properly for trips out in the cold of winter. In December 1993, Terry was starving and cold. He left his cabin for Iskut Village, a walk of almost one hundred miles. A party of Iskut men looking for him on snowmobiles to see if he was managing in the unusually cold weather found him dead.

The details of Terry's story emerge sporadically when one drives near where the men located his body. Frank Edwards points out to his children and grandchildren where certain events in Terry's last hours occurred, such as where Terry had made a small fire. Like hunting stories, these accounts are reminders about preparing properly for any activity. Iskut hunters blame Terry's death on his lack of preparedness for living in the bush during winter: Terry lacked supplies for the winter and was foolish.

Descriptions of Terry's fate also reveal concern for treating animals properly. People knew about Terry's hurting *khoh* ('grizzly bear,' *Ursus horibilis*) by attaching a plywood board with nails sticking outwards through it to the side of his trailer. Terry explained that he was protecting the trailer from the aggressive bears. A large wooden cross just off the roadway where he was found marks his life and his fate. Grizzlies often maul the memorial; large scratches are visible on the wood. According to Peter Rivers, this continuing assault was Terry's punishment for hurting grizzlies. Terry represents an anti-social individual living (at least partly) in an Iskut world where hunting and trapping are social pursuits. His actions – and the story of them – contrast with the pursuit stories of Arthur Nole and Colin Duncan, where family relationships are close to the surface. They exemplify how people replicate poor social relations in the wider world. Terry treated animals badly. He lived alone and did not share what he had. Punishment, in the form of starvation, was Terry's fate.

Stories of pursuing moose, accounts of kills, and descriptions of the mistakes of unprepared hunters make up some of the repertoire of hunting-related narratives of Iskut hunters. They are part of being *didene*. In each case, these anecdotes, which people convey seriously in everyday situations, leave outsiders such as me wondering about the details of the stories and often the point. But close analysis shows them to be rich in the symbolism of Subarctic hunting groups. They often reveal how people should treat animals. Indeed, they are allegories that explain proper relations between people, particularly where relations between moose and hunters are symbolic of relations between family members or with friends. The narratives and hunting rules here imply simply that human relationships are complex. They indicate that the obligation for people to exchange food is just as important as moose exchanging their lives for respect. Just as some moose escape, however, people do not always share food. The stories instruct audiences, then, not to be stingy while also showing that stinginess is a part of life. As with people everywhere, in Iskut Village friendships and familial relations include disappointments that future interactions usually rectify. Successful hunts follow failures, too.

4 'Rough Riding All Day': Work Animals and Guiding Work

On a sunny day in May 2002, Robert Quock and Scotty Edwards took me out to 'see the country.' We went for our drive in my noisy SUV. The men, both Iskut elders in their early seventies, were old friends of one another. Their families have history in the *Tl'abāne* and at *Tlēgōhīn*. They brought with them thermoses of tea, bag lunches, and one rifle each. We drove up the trackless BC Rail grade hoping that the summer-only road was passable this early into the spring thaw. As we travelled, we watched for animal tracks, sang along to Merle Haggard on the truck's tape player, and began building a relationship between two Iskut elders and an anthropologist – that is, we started a conversational give-and-take of identifying topics worthy of discussion. We also looked for animals; if the opportunity arose, the men wanted to kill a moose or caribou.

On this day, we drove 100 km (60 miles) up the grade in about three hours. We went past the community camp at *Kāti Chō* and into the *Tl'abāne Tū'e* valley before turning back because of deep, slushy snow on the roadway. We had an enjoyable lunch of sandwiches and tea over a fire at one of Scotty's hunting camps. After our meal, my companions set up targets and showed me how to shoot their rifles. Later, on the return trip, we spotted a lone *dih gose*, 'willow grouse,' on the road. Robert insisted that I try to shoot it. As I struggled to keep the barrel steady, it surprised me how small the bird's head looked through the sight. I missed the shot badly from about 10 m (30 feet). Robert and Scotty's friendly laughter suggested that they never expected me to hit the bird.

Throughout the day, Robert and Scotty talked at length about working for a non-Native outfitter named Tommy Walker during the 1950s. An Englishman, Walker ran a hunting outfit on the Spatsizi Plateau, at *Hok'ats Łuwe Menh*, a three or four days' walk east of Iskut Village (Walker 1976). Robert and Scotty worked for Walker for several years as wranglers, cooks, and guides. Their accounts frequently include fond memories – references to American clients, familiar trails, and work with horses. This was the era in which most Iskut families lived near *Tlēgōhīn* – the beginning of a new home at *Łuwechōn Menh*, now Iskut. From previous conversations with these men and others in Iskut Village, however, I knew of village families' mixed feelings about Walker. Walker wrote that Iskut people were 'isolated from civilization ... [and struggling] to fit into a strange environment' of cultural change when he arrived in the Spatsizi in 1948 (Walker 1976, 9; also Walker, various dates; Henderson 2006, 22–23). He was remarking on impoverished, uncivilized people unable in the face of changing economic practices to survive in a place where Tahltan speakers had lived for generations. He identified, inadvertently, challenges that had started decades earlier in Iskut history with the transition from sustenance food gathering to wage work. The rub here is that guiding required skills Iskut people had: the ability to hunt and knowledge of the land. And thus, while Iskut people remember hard times, they resent Walker's claims that he some-how saved them from disappearing further into obscurity or perhaps cultural (and physical) death. I listened for criticism of Walker as Robert and Scotty talked and found instead a focus on horses and work.

Eventually, we made it back home, empty-handed, without even a *dih*, 'chicken' (generic label for grouse). My companions did not com-ment on that as we drove back through the village, although I wondered if their wives questioned them sternly about their empty packs when they entered their houses. As I thought about our drive afterwards, I realized that some older hunters reflect on guiding work – work with domesticated animals in general – in order to comment indirectly on the changing work and food-gathering priorities of Iskut families today. Their talk is allegorical, and stories of guiding serve as com-ments on the historical and contemporary participation of Iskut people in a world that is larger than their village. They stand in contrast to the pursuit stories of Arthur Nole and Colin Duncan, but they too are cen-tral to the larger question of what it means to be *didene*.

Domesticated Animals at Iskut

A social model of human-animal relations at Iskut Village, a model that emphasizes the place of animals in Iskut social networks, works best vis-à-vis food animals. Because the social connections between food animals and people date back to myth-time, a social model is less relevant for behaviour and talk relating to domesticated and working animals, such as dogs and horses, that arrived more recently. In her review of anthropological studies of domesticated animals, Eugenia Shanklin notes that the writers emphasize ecological research showing the animals' economic value (as sustenance for people) or metaphors indicating how cultural conceptions of domesticated animals reflect social norms and order (animals as symbols of society) (Shanklin 1985, 377; also Nadasdy 2007, 29). Shanklin elaborates on the symbolic line of inquiry and the impression 'that domesticated animals occupy an intermediate position between humans (culture) and wild animals (nature)' (1985, 397). If this is true, metaphors of society that rely on domesticated animals should also exist in the middle ground between society and nature (Sharp 2001, 83).[1]

In northern Athapaskan tradition, like at Iskut Village, there is little obvious separation between culture and nature in local thought. But if the stories of recent history refer regularly to horses and dogs, it is worth considering the place of these domesticated animals in Iskut's symbolic repertoire and in the social relationships they engender. Are work animals truly different from food animals in the Iskut imagination? Do stories about horses accomplish the same goals for the narrator as accounts about moose? Is the use of domesticated animals symbolic of the modernization that paternalistic governments seek for Native people? Following Shanklin, I am curious about how all animals, including moose and horses, are 'good to think with' (Shanklin 1985, 379; cf. Levi-Strauss 1963, 89; also 1966 [1962]; Nadasdy 2007, 29), particularly in the context of narratives of historical progress and wage work that come from both Iskut people and observers from the outside who question if the traditional and their sense of the modern can co-exist.

Iskut stories that describe relations with domesticated work animals illuminate perceptions about participation in a wider world. Many of these tales include descriptions of or references to guiding non-Native hunters on trophy hunts. But memories of guiding shared as narratives are more than nostalgic reflections or commentaries on economic practices. They are statements of what Iskut people know about outsiders and how they attempt to deal with them. They can be reflections on racist attitudes by well-intentioned outsiders who wanted to remove Native people from the land to towns with schools and churches. More specifically, by evoking Tommy Walker's guiding business, the stories address indirectly Walker's idealized notions of pristine natural environments without Native people in them; for Walker, the only noble savage is one *remembered* to have lived on the land. In addition, the accounts discuss behaviour in regards to domesticated animals and outsiders and suggest specific ways to treat these animals and people. They also address the place of dogs, horses, and meddling outsiders in village life today. For Iskut audiences, memories of outsiders – human and animal – are frequently social commentaries about hunters plying their trade in new and changing circumstances.

Dogs

Are we mangy dogs to [be] kicked around? . . . Are you going to haul us back to Telegraph Creek and dump us like cattle?
— Alec Dennis, Walter L. Dennis, and Francis Louie, 22 June 1964[2]

The place of dogs in Iskut history does not always receive succinct articulation in Iskut talk or in myth-time stories. Nevertheless, the role of dogs in Iskut hunting activities, particularly traditional sustenance hunting, is apparent and important. The Tahltan Bear Dog is one of a handful of domesticated dogs indigenous to North America, and its appearance in northwestern British Columbia antedates living memories (Derr 1997, 54; Sharp 1976, 26). Teit describes its role in the Tahltan sustenance economy as being as indispensable as snowshoes (Teit 1906, 356). Dogs served Iskut hunters as pack, draft, and hunting animals until at least 1970. Some people in Iskut refer to the arrival of the first snowmobiles in the village at about that time as the beginning of the demise of the use of dogs (also Sharp 1976, 26; Nadasdy 2003, 35). Besides drafting and packing, the dogs were tenacious while hunting with their masters. Stories abound in Iskut Village about these dogs confronting bears and other animals in their dens. Iskut people are proud of the Tahltan Bear Dog, but, sadly for many people at Iskut, canine experts consider it extinct (Derr 1997, 54).[3]

Myth-time stories record the working role of dogs in sustenance hunting and their relationships with people. Tahltans at *Tlēgōhīn* and at Iskut Village know the story of the Dog Husband – a variant on a text very common throughout northern Canada.[4] In the Tahltan version, a woman marries a man who is actually a dog. The dog is part of the household, and, in the story, relationships with the dog must be thought of like those between humans. The children of the woman and the dog, pups, have incestuous relationships and overhunt the area north of *Tlēgōhīn*. As punishment for both acts, the entire family drowns trying to cross the Stikine River. The Three Sisters Rocks in the Stikine River downstream from *Tlēgōhīn* commemorate this tale.[5] Each rock represents one of the characters in the story and the place where they drowned. Thus, despite the widespread familiarity of this story in northern Canada, the Tahltan version is inscribed on the local landscape (Sheppard 1983a; Adlam 1995).

In the story of *Deneka'ladiyah*, a dog is a hunting companion.[6] The relationship between dog and hunter reflects social relations of the sort that people expect between hunting partners. The dog and hunter cooperate. Teit's version records this clearly: 'The dog ran down the goats; and when he brought them to bay, the hunter speared them' (Teit 1919, 241). As the hunt continues, however, the hunter becomes overzealous in his pursuit of an elusive goat. He scolds the goat for not giving itself up, and, because of this disrespectful talk, the hunter and his dog turn to stone (241–42). The implication is that the *Deneka'ladiyah* dog and the hunter are equally guilty of impropriety. They let each other down and fail together.

Despite its fame, few people tell the *Deneka'ladiyah* story in Iskut Village. I found that most villagers are familiar with the events it details, however, and understand it as a reminder not to hurt or talk badly about animals. Repeating the hunter's name, *Deneka'ladiyah*, is enough to convey that message. *Deneka'ladiyah* also refers to the rock formation that hunter and dog became. This commemorative rock is in the headwaters of the Spatsizi River and shows the hunter, the goat, and the dog (cf. Basso 1996). It is visible to Iskut people travelling through the Spatsizi, and hunters such as Arthur Nole say that it serves as a constant warning to hunters to act properly.

Dogs are never far from sight or mind in Iskut. Dogs come up in conversations about hunting in the old days. Some people say that packing meat from a kill to a camp is far easier with dogs than with all-terrain vehicles (ATVs). Dogs can pull sleds or carry packs along trails that are narrower and in poorer condition than ATVs can manage. I found myself experiencing at first-hand the passion for dogs and trails during an ice-fishing expedition in January. Scotty Edwards took me fishing at a hole across a snow-covered lake. We used snowshoes to get there. Once we had finished fishing, Scotty decided that I needed to learn how to 'pack a trail' like people used to do for dogs. Dogs pulled sleds behind the hunter who went ahead to pack the deep snow down enough to allow the sled to move. I spent the next hour walking back and forth over about three hundred yards of the shore, stomping down loose snow and trying to earn Scotty's approbation. I learned quickly that packing a trail was a lot of work.

Today Iskut people are ambivalent about dogs. On the one hand, they appreciate dogs for the help they have given people in the past. The Tahltan bear dog symbolizes to them their identity, particularly as it relates to hunting. They are proud of its hearty character. They speak about breeding it back into existence by mating small dogs with tough personalities. Inevitably, they will label a small and fierce dog in the village a Tahltan bear dog or compare it with the species. The Tahltan name for coyote – *tidah tlī'*, 'for nothing dog,' or an animal that is just about useless – also indicates the favour that dogs receive because they work.[7]

On the other hand, people often speak poorly about dogs. Curse words frequently include the Tahltan and the English words for dog. After a minor accident, for example, someone may utter *tlī' tsāne*, 'dog shit' in Tahltan or 'dirty dog' in English. At cards, receiving a bad hand is a *tlī'dīle*, 'dog deal,' where *dīle* represents a Tahltan pronunciation of the English word 'deal.' It looks, too, as if people treat dogs badly. The animals live outside in small shelters or under houses all year long. They seem to swelter in summer and suffer in the cold of winter. Food is fleeting for them, and many are scavengers. Feral dogs roam in the Iskut dump. In sum, Iskut dogs rarely hunt today, even though villagers still treat them like hunting dogs (also Sharp 2001, 85). Laura Rivers sums up the past and present ambivalence about dogs: 'Dogs help you, but you gotta feed them.'[8]

Horses

Telegraph Creek, BC, 8 April 1951

Dear Mr. Walker,

Please, could you buy another. 30-30 for Charlie Quock and bring it with you when you come to Cold Fish Lake. He will pay you when you come.

The horses are all right except Dart who is skinny. Seal also. All the others are fine. Only three died this winter, Montie, Glassie and Belle. Old Ronny is still alive yet.

Thank you for your letter just received. I got short of grub and came to Telegraph. Francis is feeding the horses two times a week while I am away. We got all the oats at Hyland Post.

Except for the ones mentioned above, all the horses are rolling fat. The Rasmussen horses are so wild, you cannot come near them. Queen is all right.

Hoping to see you soon, I remain yours very truly,

Alec Jack[9]

(Walker, various dates, MS-2784, box 18, file 8)

If Iskut relationships with dogs are frequently ambiguous, social and symbolic connections to horses are simply unclear. The Tahltan word for horse is *gendām*, although its origin is uncertain (John Alderete, personal communication, 1 June 2006; Angela Dennis, personal communication, October 2006); it may have Tlingit origins (Kaska Tribal Council 1997, 56). Tahltan-speaking peoples may have encountered horses first when Samuel Black visited the area (Black 1824) or perhaps later, during construction of the telegraph line north from the Stikine River towards Alaska in the 1860s. Through the end of the nineteenth century, prospectors with horses heading to the gold fields in the Yukon used this trail for an overland route within Canada.

Teit comments on use and knowledge of horses by Tahltans at *Tlēgōhīn*. Writing for Franz Boas after Teit's first trips to *Tlēgōhīn* (Thompson 2007), Teit says that horses do not much impress Tahltans: 'Although a number of Tahltan can ride and pack horses, having worked in white-man's pack-trains, etc., they are not a "horse" people, and it was said that the total number of horses owned by the tribe in the fall of 1903 was two only. For the conditions of their country, dogs are considered much more serviceable, being easily kept, and able to go over muskeg and on ground where horses could not travel. Besides, the long winters, comparative scarcity of feed, and the winter trapping excursions of the Indians, all help to prevent the keeping of horses' (Teit 1906, 346).

There is little ethnographic record of Iskut ancestors encountering horses. Naturalist Andrew Jackson Stone, who documented plants and animals in the Stikine watershed in the 1890s, travelled by foot and horse-pack train with his Tahltan guides (Stone 1896–97). Neither Emmons (1911) nor Jenness (1937) mentions horses. But Martha James says that by the 1930s 'everyone' (Iskut ancestors) had their own horse (personal communication, June 2006). Outfitters such as Steele Hyland and Walker depended on horses for their businesses. They could afford to ensure – and it was in their interest to do so – that most horses would survive the northern BC winter.

Iskut people remember Walker's horses at *Hok'ats Łuwe Menh*. As Alec Jack's letter above suggests, Iskut men cared for and monitored the condition of Walker's horses throughout the year. Their role was particularly important in winter, when Walker was absent and the horses needed considerable attention. They took these jobs seriously. In correspondence they referred to themselves as cowboys. Robert Quock continues to call himself a cowboy in reference both to his work and, light-heartedly, to his rough personality. The Iskut First Nation keeps horses today as part of the Kluachon Outfitters, a guiding business that the council runs under the direction of a non-Native person. Caring for these horses provides work for young people. Some teenagers spend their summers moving horses from the village to camps around the area and on the Spatsizi Plateau. And the jobs are reminders of how some elders made a living.

Owning and caring for horses requires earning wages from client hunters. Walker's horses are pack animals and work within the outfitting business. Unlike food animals, and as the letter above indicates, they have proper names in the tradition of farm animals and require feed. In other letters, Alec Jack describes keeping track of and at times rounding up lost horses (Walker, various dates); Robert Quock's story below describes such experiences. The actions of horses stand in contrast to the behaviours of food animals such as moose. In the bush, corrals constrain horses, which wear bells to identify their locations and are rounded up and moved as humans see fit.

There are no references to horses in Tahltan mythology, and so no mythological charter outlines proper relations with them. Unlike horses and dogs, moose find their own food. Moose punish hunters who misbehave by withholding themselves from hungry people and in doing so control the outcome of hunts. People, in contrast, punish horses that do not do as they are instructed. The stories below show that Iskut people behave differently towards horses than towards food animals. By analogy, relations with non-local people are different from those with hunting partners. Outsiders do not have a clearly defined place in the local web of life.

Transcript 4.1: Guiding Stories

Iskut associations with horses are central to guiding stories. By extension, the stories characterize the ways in which Iskut people remember, interpret, and feel about their associations with outfitters such as Tommy Walker, their client hunters, and domesticated animals. The stories speak to a different dimension of the local ecology, one in which relations between Iskut people and outsiders – people and animals – need new definitions. With an obvious focus on the guiding era of the recent past, these narratives acknowledge indirectly that relationships with food animals and hunting in the distant past have changed. Through analogy, they also offer commentary on phenomena in the present, such as mineral exploration and hydroelectric development. In my mind, these contemporary activities represent the Tommy Walkers of a new generation. The stories point to the repeated success of Iskut people at understanding the demands of outsiders and participating in new economic activities cautiously and sometimes enthusiastically. However, they also speak to the challenges of controlling the impact of outsiders on Iskut lives and sustenance traditions.

The following story is typical of others that Robert Quock told me. It is consistent with the stories that men and women often recounted while travelling around Iskut territory. It is just a few minutes in length but includes subplots and secondary accounts relating to incidents while Robert was moving horses for Tommy Walker, probably in the 1950s or 1960s. Scotty and I form the immediate audience for this story. As is often the case, the precise details of these memories are less important than the telling of the tale. The absence of broader contextual information indicates an expectation of shared history, background knowledge, and understandings of the overt and covert meanings of the text. Robert assumes that Scotty is familiar with the places and people he mentions and does not for my benefit fill in details that he omits or takes for granted. Robert provides just enough contextual material for a knowledgeable *pāne,* 'partner,' to follow along, react, and tell more stories.

[Setting: Two Iskut elders in a small SUV with an anthropologist. Llamas come into view at the side of the road. Robert Quock is speaking unless I note otherwise.]

Tahltan hunters Ben Frank and Old Dennis with Ned Brooks and client near *Tlēgōhīn*. (BC Archives and Records Service, E.01166, c. 1935; used with permission.)

Scene 1: Seeing Llamas

[A lodge owner on Eddontenajon Lake, two miles south of Iskut Village, owns a herd of llamas that he had hoped could serve in pack trips into the bush, much like horses. Iskut people say that llamas are too stubborn for such work.]

1 Dirty little animals [llamas], eh.

2 Crazy.

Scene 2: First Narrative – Rounding up Horses

3   Man horses do that.

4   Second day.   [First narrative begins]

5   They gotta go across today

6   or they gonna get it.

7   Man, then we run them down like this.

8   Two of us.

9   One on this side.

10   Just close to that river

11   that leader tried to go that way. [Horse acts improperly]

12   Wild one:

13   Go ahead

14   try to go that way.   [Horse acts improperly]

15   We hit him.   [Response to horse's decision]

16   You [Scotty Edwards] know Black Jack.

17   [SE:] Yeah.

18   That one.

19   We hit him.

20   And Silver too.

21   We, boy just . . .

22   he run to [inaudible]

23   We hit and they too

24   and then I hit him hard as I can in there.

25   After I hit side of the neck,

26   I hit him hard as I can in the rump.

27   He jumped right in the river.

28   The rest jumped.   [Horses get it right]

29 Creeks.

30 They scared of creeks.

31 Early spring,

32 them little bit of ice on the creek.

33 They wouldn't cross.

34 We make them cross that day, morning.

35 Man, I tell you,

36 we take 101 head up

37 just the two of us.

38 Up to Cold Fish.

39 I tell you, that's work.

40   And I stay at the back [trailing]

41   and he's leading them [riding point], eh.

42   Oh, go ahead of them.

43   Most of them got foal.

44   Bad ones we put down.

45   When they turn off [stop, pause?],

46   [as it was] springtime,

47   they can't.

48   They can't stay quiet cause lot of bugs.

49   They have to ring their bell, eh.

50   I know when they get out,

51   I get them on the road, trail again.

52   Man, by time we get to camp,

53   we're both played out, boy.

54   Rough riding all day.

55   Chasing horses.

56   [Tad:] Wow. That's a lot of work.

57   It is.

[Scene summary: This is the recent past when animals require and accept guidance from humans; llamas are the horses of the current era.]

Scene 3: Confrontation

58   One time we stayed Mink Creek.

59   Thirteen days we stayed there.

60   Scotty know that place, Mink Creek.

61   Took all the horses.   [Second narrative begins]

62   We took that 101 head.

63   Bill and Johnny all help us to get there.

64   And we supposed to look after them until they catch us up.

65   Holy man,

66   thirteen days we stayed there

67   and them old people never came up.

68   And them horses went back.

69   We didn't know.

70   We hunt them all over the country.

71   I don't know how many days,

72   My partner got bad head.

73   'I'll get down there and take your guts out with my knife.'

74   I go,

75   I grab his knife.

76   'Come on down,'

77   I say.

78   'Cut me open.'   [Symbolically similar to moose sacrifice]

79   Man, from there he never talk to me.

80   I didn't say it.

[Scene summary: A hunter acts like a sacrificial moose.]

Scene 4: Resolution of Wrangling Problems

81   And that's the day I find them horses.

82   I went down,   [Third narrative begins]

83   I went up Scotty Creek.

84   I come back out.

85   I'm making tea.

86   Here I hear a bunch of horse bell coming up.

87   Bill and them got them halfway, heh.

88   Westevan Creek.

89   From there they come up.

90   Man, a lot of horses.

91   I wait.

92   I just keep counting, counting.

93   The last one went by.

94   I wait a little while

95   and then I dump my teapot

96   and I swing in the saddle.

97   I'm on my way.

98   I go behind them

99   and I holler like hell. [Addressing the herd and his companion]

100   Man I was glad I got them all.

101   We got them all again.

102   Chased them uphill.

103   I hear my partner holler ahead of me.

104   Here, he wait.

105   'Ho.'

106   We start chasing them back.

107   Man, 'way we go.

[Scene summary: Hunters will manage today and into the future as they always did.]
[Robert turns in truck and comments to Scotty Edwards in back seat about the small SUV.]

108   Too small, huh, *pāne*?

(24 May 2002)

Textual Considerations

Imagine how Robert's account begins. The three of us are in my noisy truck. The truck is small and somewhat uncomfortable, and yet we are all glad to be leaving the village for a few hours. The tape recorder is running, and country music is on the stereo. As we round a corner on the highway within a mile of Iskut Village, llamas appear on the side of the road. They are tied to posts in the ground and are simply relaxing in the weak sun. Robert comments immediately: 'Dirty little animals, eh / Crazy' (lines 1–2). Robert then launches into a story about how horses are as stubborn as llamas. Scene 1 blends several incongruous images, at least as far as conventional ideas go about hunting in northern Canada. Two elders and I talk within range of a tape recorder taped to a bench in my uncomfortable truck. They accept the fact that I am going to use the conversations for some project in the future. We spot llamas. Robert's disgust is apparent. Moose are not spoken about this way. It is unclear to me why llamas are both dirty and crazy. Scene 1 establishes immediately the density of this text before the narrative patterns become obvious.

As scene 2 begins, llamas are fresh in our minds. The animals are the property of a non-Native lodge owner who intended to use them on trail walks with tourists. The llamas often provoke snickering or snide commentary when Iskut people pass them: llamas are strange, inedible creatures that are out of place. They have never fulfilled their promise as pack animals, and there is a general feeling that Iskut people knew better than to use them in a place where horses, dogs, and humans are far more effective for all types of work. By extension, Iskut knowledge of the bush is superior to that of a non-Native businessman who thinks that llamas will be useful in this country.

Robert's text departs from this comparison into an account of an indeterminate trip in which he remembers his days as a wrangler. The story opens on the second day of that trip (line 4), and Robert identifies a second person he is with (line 8). He describes forcing horses to cross a small river when they are unwilling to do so. He conveys a great deal of the temperament and character of the guiding horses: they are stubborn and prone to individualistic actions, such as wandering off or going their own way (line 11 and 14), and creeks scare them.

Robert's first account also reveals the relationship between wranglers and horses. Horses are subject to harsh treatment and obvious punishment by humans if they do not behave or act as the wrangler wishes. Robert describes hitting the horses in order to force them to do what *he* wants: 'After I hit the side of the neck, / I hit him hard as I can in the rump / He jumped right in the river' (lines 25–27). This part of the story finishes as it began, with further reflection back on the difficulty of getting horses to cross rivers (lines 29–34). Like llamas, and unlike dogs and moose, horses are not indigenous to the area, and working with them can result in misunderstandings between rider and beast.

As scene 2 progresses, Robert develops the comparison between llamas and horses. By doing so, he begins an evaluation of the guiding era through analogy and implicit comparison with hunting for food in both the distant past and today. Both llamas and horses require care and guidance from humans. Robert makes this clear in the narrative when he states two instances of the horses acting improperly: first, Robert says 'Just close to that river / that leader tried to go that way [away from the river]' (lines 10–11); and second, 'Wild one: / Go ahead / try to go that way' (lines 12–14). After working at it, by hitting Black

Jack for example (lines 15–16), Robert convinces the horses to cross the creek. He elaborates: 'I hit him hard as I can in the rump. / He jumped right in the river. / The rest jumped' (lines 26–28); the horses 'get it' right after a significant effort on Robert's part. In sum, scene 2 develops from the sight of llamas acting lazily. The animals provoke comments about horses that act improperly in the recent and remembered past. The speaker implies a contrast with hunting for food in the distant past (and possibly in the present) when food animals behaved according to rules that mirrored the respect that hunters – and all consumers of animal flesh – showed them.

The second half of scene 2 also focuses on moving horses. Here, Robert is more specific. He is leading 101 horses to *Hok'ats Łuwe Menh*, the base camp of Tommy Walker's guiding operations (line 38), and says that he has one partner (line 37). The horses wear bells to identify their location, further differentiating them from moose (line 49). Similarly, Robert and his partner put down 'bad' foals (line 43–44) – presumably sick or injured animals. The death of horses reflects not a specific hunter-prey relationship here but a utilitarian connection between labourer and livestock. Thus hands control even the lives of horses by feeding or killing them, which is unthinkable and impossible vis-à-vis moose, at least where traditional knowledge about the agency of moose is concerned.

Robert explains how he accomplishes this work: 'And I stay at the back / and he's leading them, eh' (lines 40–41). The endeavour is hard and tiring: 'Man, by the time we get to camp, / we're both played out, boy / Rough riding all day. / Chasing horses' (lines 52–55). Like moose-hunting stories, these accounts of guiding emphasize bush travel. Unlike accounts of hunting moose, however, they represent manual and pastoral labourers who move horses in response to the employer, incoming clients, the animals, or the seasons.

The guiding stories also indicate how Iskut people confronted potential ideological problems, not to mention power imbalances, in relation to disrespecting animals in the context of hunting for cash. Hunting for sport was relatively new in the 1950s, and, unlike hunting for food, killing for trophies seems disrespectful of the prey, be it moose, caribou, or sheep (also Scott and Webber 2001). Iskut hunters do not have any reservations, however, about hunting for wages. Operating as a wage hunter is, as an Iskut elder explained to me, quite different from sustenance hunting. I interpret this to mean that hunting for a wage is work in a separate domain of life from sustenance hunting, in which spiritual connections to animals are paramount. It relates instead to a Christian work ethic and human domination of animals. It seems reasonable to assume that wage hunters can speak badly of animals with impunity – even if he also hunts for sustenance – although I have no textual evidence to support this assumption.[10]

Scene 3 occurs at and near Mink Creek, a camp close to the outfitter's camp at *Hok'ats Łuwe Menh* (line 58). It develops quickly after I indicate my amazement at the amount of work that employees of the guide outfitters do (line 56). Robert draws Scotty into the story near the beginning by noting Scotty's familiarity with the Mink Creek camp (line 60). It is unclear if he states this line for Scotty's benefit or for mine; it holds Scotty's interest by broadening Robert's personal account to include experiences common to both men.

Now Robert moves away from comparisons of work animals and implicit commentaries on the hunting past. Here he confronts directly the difficulty of managing animals and his workmates. His help does not arrive: 'Holy man,' says Robert, drawing out the word 'holy,' 'thirteen days we stayed there / and them old people never came up. / And those horses went back. / We didn't know, / We hunt them all over the country' (lines 65–70). Keeping track of time is an obsession for Robert, who notes twice that he and his partner were at Mink Creek for thirteen days (lines 59 and 66), only to say in his next breath that he did not know how many days they were in the bush. Working as a guide required him to pay attention to a clock in order to meet the needs of transient client hunters and the schedules that Walker established at base camp. Work has not gone as they planned, and Robert directs his frustration more at his human companions and the ubiquitous nature of clock-time than at his animal help.

The story centres on rounding up horses after they escaped from Robert and his companion. The men had been tending the animals while waiting for help from the clients, which did not come for nearly two weeks. Robert says that the horses headed back to the main camp after thirteen days at the bush camp, where they were probably in a small and simple bush corral. The hard life of working in the bush comes through in this story. Robert reiterates the thirteen-day duration of the stay at Mink Creek, which included several days of rounding up the horses after they decided to move back home on their own (lines 70–71). The statement that 'them old people never came up' (line 67) seems to convey frustration, as does the fact that finding the horses took so long that Robert could not remember how many days it was (line 71). Later, in scene 4, Robert notes that Bill and Johnny showed up, but made it only halfway (line 87); they did help recover some horses, but Robert reiterates that there were a lot of horses on the move (lines 90–93). This is bush work, but of a new sort. Iskut men were excellent guides because they knew the bush so well. They could find animals, knew trails, and understood how to kill and butcher game. They applied this knowledge, however, for the recreation of outsiders and because they wanted and needed to participate in a local, small-scale wage economy.

Central to scene 3 is the dialogue between Robert and his sick partner, which the dramatic knifing moment resolves. The exchange is an example of what Robert calls his 'cowboy life.' In the scene, Robert says that his partner has a 'bad head' (line 72). I assume that the man was hungover, although possibly something else ailed him. Robert then reports his partner's first words: 'I'll take you down there and take your guts out with my knife' (line 73). Here, Robert engages the threat: 'I grab his knife. / "Come on down," / I say. / "Cut me open"' (lines 75–78). This rebuttal puts the man in his place, and their communication and connection end (line 79).

Through scene 4, the historical eras and changing relations between men and animals emerge more obviously. The men move the horses: 'Ho. / We start chasing them back. / Man, 'way we go' (lines 105–7); just as in the hunting past and in the present, the men have managed changing times and new economic ventures. They can take significant roles in the new guiding industry, and, as they assert today, it was the efforts of men such as Robert and Scotty that allowed Tommy Walker to run a profitable enterprise. The meanings of these scenes are subtle, but a closer reading shows that hunting had been successful, guiding worked well in the recent past, and new activities or intrusions into the area will prosper today. As the story ends, there is optimism about adjusting to changing circumstances.

After the job, Robert's account shifts from first-person plural to first-person singular, suggesting that he finished up on his own. He looks out for himself and completes the work without direction from anyone else. It is not until after he fights with his partner that he finds the horses. He draws clearly the connection between cause and effect, indicating that the fight required resolution before his work could succeed. Even when Bill and Johnny arrive, he waits until the horses pass him before rising: 'I wait a little while / and then I dump my teapot / and I swing in the saddle' (lines 94–96). He then claims credit for having rounded up the horses himself, before pluralizing the verb and returning to an inclusive account: 'Man I was glad I got them all. / We got them all again' (lines 100–1). He reconnects with his partner, and they begin working together again (lines 103–7). The stories speak to relationships between hands and exemplify one way in which personal history illustrates the community history of new encounters with non-Natives.

The tale ends abruptly: 'Too small, huh, *pāne*' (line 108). The meaning of this comment is unclear although it is likely meant for Scotty about the size of my truck. Once again, these men know more about what works best – and I should really have a better vehicle. 'Huh, *pāne*' emphasizes Robert's observations about the truck and possibly prompts Scotty's validation of the statement. Robert may be asking for someone in the know to corroborate the sorts of events in his accounts. Scotty did not respond immediately with a guiding or 'hard work' story of his own, but later during our trip he weighed in with personal examples.

Managing the Past for a Political Present

Guiding stories deal mostly with conditions of wage work. In them, the economic changes that have come to northwestern British Columbia in the lifetimes of Iskut people are debated. They describe an era when new opportunities confronted Iskut hunters and newcomers brought different ideas about how to use land and animals. In many ways, the guiding economy of the 1950s replicates the hunting economy of the distant past. Stories of guiding show, for example, that guiding is compatible with gathering food as both pursuits require many of the same skills. Iskut employees played a substantial role in the success of guiding businesses. Today people convey guiding history verbally as a way of discussing recent injustices and, as I suggest below, rhetorically controlling intrusions into Iskut lands (also Scott and Webber 2001, 163).[11]

Guiding stories are also personal narratives of participation in big-game guiding, a historically significant industry in the BC north (Sheppard 1983b; also Loo 2001a, b, 2006). By extension, Iskut narratives of this era explore their families' past at a time of profound changes in local economic practices. With trapping, killing animals became commercial, mercantile. This process continued with guiding, and Iskut people were good at it.[12] Guiding stories are told locally and the audiences are largely Iskut people. Stories of this sort validate individual credibility, hunting knowledge, and the collective experiences of a broader Iskut community. Evoking this past is also a measure of pride. The stories relate the important roles of Iskut men and women in the guiding business, which required their expert hunting knowledge. They also represent nostalgia for an era when Iskut people contributed extensively to the northern BC economy. To younger generations facing a growing range of employment or lifestyle choices today, these stories illustrate the potential for hunting skills and the continuing value of these activities.

Robert's guiding stories illuminate social relations within Iskut Village and outside it. Robert directs the narrative above to his lifelong friend Scotty Edwards. He shares similar guiding experiences in much the same way that Colin and John shared hunting stories in chapter 3. Robert's and Scotty's families, however, have as widely different histories as is possible in Iskut. Robert remembers life at *Łuwechōn* and married into a *Me'etsendāne* and Commonage family. Scotty's ancestors are Tahltan and Gitksan, and his wife is from a prominent family at *Tlēgōhin*. They grew up with both dogs and horses. The shared experiences and friendships of guiding reveal a common link for people with disparate backgrounds living at Iskut. Friends talk about good and bad times while working in the bush. Such conversation reminds speakers and listeners that common experiences, even fifty years in the past, are the basis for continuing relationships today.

Talk of guiding also reflects changing ideas about familial obligations. Guiding made earning cash and buying equipment important for men like Scotty and Robert. As the epigraph above suggests, guiding men realized that they could take more than meat to their families. Just as acting like a cowboy is central to Robert's personal identity even today, his ability to make money enhanced his reputation during the 1950s. In this regard, my presence at his presentation is notable. It became evident early on that talking about the guiding past with me was appropriate. Robert may even have intended part of his story for me. His account of wage work reminded me that an economy of sustenance food gathering was largely history in Iskut. Robert distances himself from the potential stigma of hunting for a living and by doing so identifies himself as a person who enjoys making money.

In the middle of the narrative, we see Robert's rough encounter with his guiding partner and his ability to control that man. Like a moose and its control of the hunt by the choice it makes to sacrifice itself to respectful hunters (chapter 3), Robert controls his unruly partner. Robert's story may be, in fact, a broader effort to incorporate Walker and his client hunters into the social networks of friends and rivals, insiders and outsiders, for the story moves gently between appreciation of the work and disdain for its challenges (also Scott and Webber 2001).[13] This commentary resonated for me, even at the time. It suggests obliquely that Robert saw some other people as a threat to him and perhaps to his ability to earn an income or to maintain a high standard of work. He told me as much in more direct terms months later when he warned me that he would stop working with me if I spent time with rival Iskut families. I was an outsider, a newcomer, and an anthropologist, and Robert was managing me as if I was a new guiding partner.

There is no single narrative about guiding at Iskut despite the common threads and non-Native protagonists. Each teller speaks about the events of that era in light of his or her own experiences. These stories do generate discussion and reinterpretation through the rebuttal of individual stories with other accounts. Robert, for example, speaks of his own experience, but the elements within this genre are consistent, and Scotty can reply with his own versions. Each account has its own authority, which says that an individual was there and participated. Collectively, the stories reflect an era in the recent past during which hunting activities, hunting knowledge, and ritual relationships between hunter and prey were shifting from an emphasis on sustenance to earning wages. Still, as in the pursuit stories in chapter 3, older elements are recast in new circumstances. Guiding stories, then, permit a discussion of the past and affiliation with a common history in a place where such talk can be problematic. In this history, as noted above, some voices are louder than others. The guiding stories relate common experiences and provide a sense of solidarity – to paraphrase Anthony D. Smith (1981) — in a place where shared history is sometimes hard to see. Elements of Iskut ethnic identity are in play despite the lack of a common narrated event.

Further, by telling guiding stories, Iskut people make their own history more visible. The accounts demonstrate, for example, these residents' historical connections to the Spatsizi Plateau and the *Tl'abāne*. They show that Iskut people did not give up hunting traditions simply because they started earning a wage and using horses. Instead, the traditions of hunting allowed Iskut people to affiliate with the new guiding industry easily and successfully; the idea of remaining *didene* despite changing traditions endures in these episodes. Now, as Iskut leaders learn how to use their history to illustrate their claims on local lands, and to refute the claims of others, documentation of this history will come into greater demand. These leaders understand the litigious provincial and Canadian systems, which demand proof of historical ties to specific places. Guiding stories may offer this proof, but courts have not yet tested them. Likewise, these stories may simply add to mainstream Canadian ideas about Native cultures that disappeared or changed into something else long ago. At the very least, the reflections on local history in the narratives of Robert Quock help other Canadians understand that Iskut people do not shun change.

5   Chief Louie's Speech at Spatsizi Plateau Wilderness Park

... collective names are a sure sign and emblem of ethnic communities, by which they distinguish themselves and summarize their 'essence' to themselves – as if in a name lay the magic of their existence and guarantee of their survival.

—Anthony D. Smith, *The Ethnic Origin of Nations* (1986), 23

A Reunion Camp on the Spatsizi Plateau

In May 2004, a buzz went through the Iskut community. Every member of the small Aboriginal group at Iskut Village, British Columbia, received an invitation to go camping at *Hok'ats Łuwe Meṅh* in the heart of the Spatsizi Plateau Wilderness Park. With a little digging and after my own formal invitation arrived in the mail, I learned that the Collingwoods, an outfitting family who guide hunters in the park, were working with elected leaders of the Iskut First Nation to fly Iskut families into the park. 'The Return of the *Tl'ogot'ine*, The Long Grass People, To the Land of Their Ancestors,' as the invitation billed it, involved a memorial event celebrating the origins of some Iskut families on the Spatsizi Plateau. The Iskut First Nation also wanted to remember the work of dozens of Tahltan-speaking peoples in the guiding industry during the 1950s and 1960s. The Collingwoods' website advertised the event as an opportunity for adventure seekers and cultural tourists to meet Iskut elders, eat wild game, and experience Native culture.

The Iskut First Nation and the Collingwoods also invited thirty additional guests to attend free of charge or by voluntary donation. Outsiders attending included government administrators and scientists, journalists, explorer and Iskut friend Wade Davis, noted environmentalist David Suzuki, academics, and leaders from neighbouring Native groups. *Hok'ats Łuwe Menh* is an important place in Iskut history. As the location of a guide-outfitting camp that renowned big-game hunter Tommy Walker built, it is where Iskut hunting traditions intersect with the development of a northern wage economy (see Loo 2006). For twenty years, from 1948 to 1968, Walker hosted big-game hunters from around the world. He employed numerous Iskut and other Tahltan-speaking people as guides, cooks, and wranglers. Walker is an ambivalent figure in Iskut history. Many Iskut residents respect him for employing so many Aboriginal people but resent him for suggesting in his memoirs that the Iskut families were struggling to survive when he arrived in the Spatsizi region (Walker 1976, 133–35, 165). Many Iskut people are also still angry that Walker helped facilitate their relocation from the Spatsizi to the regional centre at *Tlēgōhīn* during the 1950s (Walker, various dates, 1976; Henderson 2006).

During the weekend reunion camp, Iskut Chief Louis Louie told me that Walker encouraged the move to keep them from hunting and fishing in the Spatsizi; he wanted to keep the game for himself (Louis Louie, personal communication, 24 July 2004; also Henderson 2006; Pynn 2006). The Indian agent and the priests at *Tlēgōhīn* also played a role in the relocation from the Spatsizi Plateau. They pressed Iskut families to move permanently to *Tlēgōhīn* largely because it made their own lives easier (Walker to Federal Indian Commissioner, 10 October 1950, in Walker, various dates); families could attend church and children could go to school without the priests having to travel so much (Sheppard 1983b, 14–15).

The invitation to this trip thrilled me. I had heard lots of stories of *Hok'ats Łuwe Menh*, Tommy Walker, horse wrangling, and the Spatsizi. I wanted to see the place for myself. I might hear more accounts of a critical era in the history of Iskut in a mixed and varied audience. I suspected that being at *Hok'ats Łuwe Menh* would provoke historical talk among attendees. As it turned out, I heard direct talk about the past and much more. Iskut's hunting culture came to the surface that weekend, and strategies for discussing the past carefully – distancing, allusion, and synecdoche – were on display too.

On the day of the trip to *Hok'ats Łuwe Menh*, I went to the float-plane dock at *Tatāge Menh*, a ten-minute drive south of Iskut Village. The plane was an 'Otter' capable of carrying nine passengers and landing on lakes throughout the area. Some of the Iskut families travelled on the flight. Other non-Natives also filled seats on the plane. On the forty-minute trip, I learned of the Iskut people's excitement about seeing a place they had heard about so many times but had never visited. The Eaglenest Mountains we crossed were extremely rugged. Having driven along the edge of this range dozens of times in 2002 and having heard the descriptions of elders travelling through it on foot and horseback, I found its seeming impassability overwhelming. The need for an extensive trail network through the mountain passes was clear from above, and the value of experts' tracking skills and knowledge of the area was obvious.

After landing on *Hok'ats Łuwe Menh*, I surveyed the camp. A dozen cabins or so sit on the side of a steep embankment rising abruptly out of the north end of the lake. Iskut elders and families had already claimed the sleeping cabins. The rest of us pitched self-standing, tourist tents on the highest terrace above the lake. In a neat historical reversal, this was the terrace where Iskut families had stayed at Walker's insistence during the 1950s. He had not permitted them to live in the main camp, and now they relegated us to their former spot.[1]

A variety of events and activities occurred during the weekend. Family groups hiked up nearby mountains or into mountain passes with historically significant names such as *Dane'hih* and Airplane Valley. Some of us went on a horseback trip that the Collingwoods had organized. The children swam in the lake, some fished from shore, and we played stick games after dinner. I joined Iskut people playing cards each evening, as I had done so many times during my fieldwork. We played cards discreetly, however, usually waiting until most people were in bed. Only then did we turn on flashlights and pull out sacks of quarters to gamble in the near-darkness of the cooking cabin. The participants thought that gambling with cards would spoil the illusion of a 'traditional camp' for the other guests. The non-Iskut weekenders participated in any or all events as they desired. A few joined in the stick games, but most preferred to watch. Some of them hiked together and relaxed in their own cohorts. At times, the split between Native and non-Native groups was very obvious, though understandable, as neither group knew the other very well.

It was apparent early on that the Iskut people were enjoying this event. Socially and culturally, it was a tremendous opportunity to take children to a place with which all Iskut families and most elders associate intense emotions and memories. Likewise, many of the Iskut adults had not been back to *Hok'ats Łuwe Menh* since the provincial park was created in the mid-1970s. The trip was a homecoming for them. It also allowed leaders to endorse publicly the Collingwoods and their guiding business. This increased the role of the Iskut First Nation in decisions that the Collingwoods made in the park, and, by financing much of the event, the Collingwoods gained favour with the Iskut First Nation.

There were good political reasons for the trip too. It was a chance for Iskut people to take a public stage and raise community concerns about hunting rights and park access. Because the attendees included a former provincial minister and current administrators from BC Parks, the trip gave the chief and the band council a forum to remind the politicians that the Iskut people had lived in the area before it was a park and, indeed, long before Walker appeared on the scene. They could talk directly and openly about the alienation from the park that many in their community felt. And the trip showed that they were willing to visit and use park lands – to be a presence there – even if they felt physical and emotional distance from them on account of provincial management. The fact that the Iskut First Nation had never relinquished its rights to park lands through any formal treaty with the BC government provided a compelling background to the assertions of ownership that its members' presence represented.

Transcript 5.1: Louis Louie's Speech at *Hok'ats Łuwe Menh*

This chapter explores the ideas of Iskut people about their history as they have emerged in a public performance. Specifically, I analyse a speech by elected chief Louis Louie to Iskut and non-Native guests at *Hok'ats Łuwe Menh* (Figure 7) on 24 July 2004. Following Hymes (1981), I take performance to mean a stylized presentation requiring insiders to have special knowledge in order to understand and interpret the presentation (Hymes 1981, 79): 'Performance has reference to the realization of known traditional material, but the emphasis is on the constitution of a social event, quite likely with emergent properties ... The concern is with performance ... as something creative, realized, achieved, even transcendent of the ordinary course of events' (80–81). To label this a performance accepts that Chief Louie is speaking in an appropriate form; this is a political speech by an elected Native leader at a celebratory event that draws together Native and non-Native people. One additional point from Hymes: '[A] performance [is a] cultural behavior for which a person assumes responsibility to an audience' (84). As I detail below, Chief Louie faced multiple audiences, and he assumed responsibility to speak directly to many of them.

During my time living and researching in Iskut, I came to recognize that the composition of a group called Iskut was often in flux.[2] In some situations, such as during resource negotiations with the provincial government, an assertion of ethnicity under a single name or ethnonym, such as 'Iskut' or 'Tahltan,' marks group solidarity in Iskut Village.[3] Acknowledging the possibility that Iskut is a single ethnic group is important for Iskut people and bureaucrats because it is central to claims of land and Aboriginal rights.[4] To have a legitimate claim, a Native group must demonstrate something like ethnic identity to the government, courts, and resource-extraction companies. Still, I have never seen anything at Iskut besides ambivalence towards the idea of a unified ethnic identity. Indeed, my analysis of Chief Louie's speech shows that the Iskut group sometimes looks like an ethnic group and at other times does not. Yet I cannot say that the group ceases to exist at times when an ethnic identity is unclear. People share a focus on hunting and perhaps on Walker, but these are not the focal points for a singular Iskut ethnicity that outsiders expect. There is no common origin myth because families have diverse histories. Chief Louie pointed directly and indirectly to all these issues in his talk at *Hok'ats Łuwe Menh*.

In the speech, Chief Louie used his rhetorical prowess to generate a powerful expression of the connections between his family, his community, Walker, and the Spatsizi Plateau. Of particular interest to me – and to the study of how Iskut people see their community's composition – is his use of *Tl'ogot'ine*. This is a seldom-heard, but ethnographically and historically dense ethnonym relating to some Iskut families. Some Iskut people use it today in response to increasing claims on land and resources by outsiders in northern British Columbia. Chief Louie's use of this moribund label asserted political and legal control over the Spatsizi; he reclaimed the park largely on the basis of naming the ancestral group that lived there.

The formal celebrations of the *Hok'ats Łuwe Menh* weekend took place on a hot, sunny Saturday afternoon. We gathered on a large, flat terrace about seventy-five feet above the lake with tourist tents all round, the space to which Walker relegated the Iskut people more than a half-century earlier. There, we listened to speeches by members of each Iskut family. Chief Louie also spoke on behalf of the entire community. He had held his position for most of the past thirty years (he

Chief Louis Louie speaks before assembled guests at *Hok'ats Łuwe Menh*. He wears a button blanket depicting a wolf crest. The bushes in front of Chief Louie cover up a plaque and sculpture, both of which were unveiled later in the ceremony. (Photograph by Robert N. Diaz; used with permission.)

retired in 2005). Throughout his tenure, he represented the community in political dealings with 'foreign' politicians. He remains a visible representative, now the patriarch, of a large family with origins on the Spatsizi Plateau.

Chief Louie addressed the crowd wearing a coastal-style black-and-red button blanket depicting a wolf crest (Figure 7). The regalia marked him as a member of the Wolf Clan and, lest anyone be unsure, as a Native person. While he welcomed the guests warmly, his tone was serious. He filled his presentation with passion for the Spatsizi region. And he noted the importance of the *Hok'ats Łuwe Menh* camp for him, his relatives, and dozens of other Tahltan-speaking people. Notably, he described its history, from the distant past to the present, in the clearest terms I have ever heard.

I present the speech in its entirety (transcript 5.1). In the transcription, I have aligned the text to accentuate and emphasize the two primary historical eras to which the speaker refers. Text to the left is about the present and for the audience of Iskut people and visitors. The text one column to the right describes action that occurred in the guiding era of the recent past. I acted as master of ceremonies at this event. Robert N. Diaz, a graduate student in history at the time and my long-time collaborator on Tahltan land-use projects, recorded the speeches with a video camera. This transcript comes from that video tape.

The Speech

[Setting: The afternoon is sunny and hot. A group of about seventy-five people have gathered in a circle around a glacial erratic covered with brush. Iskut First Nation Chief Louis Louie addresses the crowd.]

1   Good afternoon
2   ladies and gentlemen, elders and children.
3   We are home at last.
4   After forty years absent from our home,
5   we have returned.
    This is the land of the *Tl'ogot'ine*
    Our forefathers has held this land for us
    and it's one outfitter that came in here in the first place
    and say we had no claim to this land.
10   We made him look good.
I hate to speak ill of the dead,
but the truth gotta be known.
It gotta be straightened out
that we were the first people here.
15   You look around on the trails,
you'll find obsidian.
Arrowheads.
My son worked,
my two sons worked for the parks
20   a couple of years back
And they brought a lot of arrowheads home.

And we can return.
We gotta preserve for our future generations
so they can come back here
25   and celebrate like we done now.
And they are going to be in partnership with various groups of
                        people in here,
so that we will always be connected to this great land.

      I spend ten years here guiding for these people in here.
      And it's not because of the money.
30   I make better money working on the construction on the
      highway.
      I was makin' $25,
      but me and my five brothers
      came back here every summer,
      in August,
35   for the country
      and for the lifestyle.
      We was making $250 a month,
      compared to $2,500 we made on the highway.
      Just for the land.
40   And we all gotta remember our elders who have passed on
      before us.
      Like Peter Dennis
      who spent thirty or forty years guiding in this outfit.
      Robert Quock cooked for them.
      Husband of Jenny Quock.
45   All the grandchildren are here.
      Charles, Charles Quock.   [Wind picks up]
      Charlie Abou.

[Recording is inaudible because of wind for 8s]

      . . . only one who stayed behind with Tommy Walker

[Recording is inaudible because of wind for 3s]

      during the winter,
50   and guided with Tommy Walker.

There was one of my colleagues,
told me just this morning
wanting to get a meeting scheduled.
He . . . say that the Tahltan has no connection to this land,
55   which is not true.
>   If it wasn't for our people
>   I doubt Tommy Walker would have ever reached this place.
>   And it's one of our elders that passed on too
>   he brought here.
60   He brought him here.
>   He was only 18 at the time.
You see,
>   Tommy Walker had a lot of influence in Victoria at that time.
>   He got someone in there
65   with a lot of decision making on his behalf.
>   And when he went through Caribou Hide
>   and Metsantan
>   and all over here,
>   there was a lot of people
70   who thought he was the first white man.
>   There was numerous white man before Tommy Walker
>   got here.

[wind subsides]
Hyland Post
and all those people up in this region.
Why Tommy Walker did, don't want us in here
75   was because he saw us as competition
>   for the wildlife in this country
>   Where we live by it
>   and our forefathers lived by it too.
That's why they call us the nomads
80   because we don't stay one place.
We always move with the migration of the animals.
Now that we settle down
we still get lonesome for this land.
And I . . .   [sentence unfinished]
85   maybe it's really good idea that we can pause for a minute of silence
>   for all of our elders.

[Pause 13 seconds]

I'm sure all our elders looking at us today
are really glad we've come down
to reclaim our place in this land.
And I would like to thank Ray Collingwood
90   and all those who were involved.
Sally Havard.
And Danielle [Boissevain].
It took a lot of hard work to make this possible.
To make this a huge success.
95   We have more speeches coming on
and it's getting hot in this blanket.   [Laughter]
Let's keep it very short.
Thank you.

[Applause]
(24 July 2004)

Textual Considerations

In the speech, Chief Louie claims a long history for Iskut people on the Spatsizi Plateau. Central to the performance is his initial assertion that he is revising history: 'I hate to speak ill of the dead / but the truth gotta be known.[5] / It gotta be straightened out / that we were the first people here' (lines 11–14). He continues by reminding listeners that Tommy Walker's arrival interrupted what was otherwise a continuous occupation of the Spatsizi Plateau (line 7). Still, Walker's business was a success because of help from Iskut people (line 10). And Chief Louie cleverly notes that it was an Iskut ancestor who brought Walker to the Spatsizi in the first place (lines 59–60).

The Iskut families are the central audience for Chief Louie. They receive his speech with applause. He directs many of his statements at them. He says, for example, 'Our forefathers has held this land for us' (line 7), and his use of the first-person-plural pronoun 'our' draws Iskut people into his rhetoric. He constructs much of the rest of the speech around references to the guiding era and specific people who worked in the industry, mixing group history with personal experience. The non-Iskut guests make up a second audience. The chief's plural pronouns exclude non-Natives from some of his talk; 'our' forefathers, after all, did not visit the Spatsizi until very recently. With the separation of audiences that his words create, each group receives different messages about land ownership and local history.

Chief Louie's flannel button blanket marks specific choices about the history and identity on display for all his audiences. These objects are ceremonial regalia from the Pacific coast, emerging probably from contact with Tlingit people, who associate them with hereditary dances and potlatches. Iskut ancestors would probably not have worn them before associating with *Tlēgōhīn* Tahltans and coastal Tlingits. The blankets are uncomfortable in the heat (line 96) and not precisely Iskut. I have, however, seen Iskut people wear them in conjunction with Athapaskan hide-and-bead slippers or bags, having restyled them and made them their own. Button blankets represent the marginalization of Iskut people who do not have their own distinct symbols. Still, there is pragmatism to adopting traditions. Native and non-Native people recognize coastal regalia and see them as a pan-Native symbol of Aboriginality. These objects assist Iskut people to assert their rights publicly. And they have been in use in Iskut for generations.

A number of Chief Louie's rhetorical techniques and narrative subsections assert the role of Iskut families at *Hok'ats Łuwe Menh* and on the Spatsizi Plateau. He begins by identifying the trip's importance using words that indicate that he (and probably others) has been thinking of this day for some time: 'We are home at last. / After forty years absent from our home, / we have returned. / This is the land of the *Tl'ogot'ine'* (lines 3–6). He evokes specific historical references here. Forty years earlier, Iskut people had moved away from the Spatsizi Plateau, about the time of the founding of the contemporary village at Iskut.

The reference to the *Tl'ogot'ine* (line 6) is what I find most remarkable in this speech. Most experts assume that they are the ancestral group that lived on the plateau (Teit 1912–15a, b; Jenness 1937, 13). The name means 'Grassy [Meadow] People,' where *tl'oyh* is grassy meadow and *got'ine* is people.[6] A second ancestral group is prominent in Iskut – the *Tl'abānot'ine*, or the 'People of *Tl'abāne*.' Their homeland is the *Tl'abāne* – the headwaters of *Hok'āz Tū'e* (and *Tl'abāne Tū'e*) southwest of the wilderness park. But why did Chief Louie make no reference to the *Tl'abānot'ine*?

I did not hear *Tl'ogot'ine* during my dissertation fieldwork and noted a reference to the Long Grass People only once. I suspect that the term was rarely in use in the village at that time, perhaps because people found little need for such detailed reflections of ancestry and origins during a time of relative political calm. So why, in 2004, does this label appear publicly? It gives the speaker a precise ethnic label that ties some Iskut people to the Spatsizi Plateau. Chief Louie's speech is instantly inclusive of a range of people with connections to the plateau. Moreover, because he avoids labels such as Iskut and Tahltan, his words do not restrict claims to this place to inhabitants of the contemporary Iskut, *Tlēgōhīn*, or *Tatl'ah* villages. Rather, they emphasize connections to a particular spot through ancestry.[7]

The label *Tl'ogot'ine* excludes Tahltan-speaking peoples without ancestry on the Spatsizi. Some of these Natives live in Iskut Village. Further analysis of attendance at *Hok'ats Łuwe Menh* makes Chief Louie's choices in the speech notable. All Tahltan-speaking families participated in guiding work. Yet all but two of the family groups who made public presentations that weekend were headed by close relatives and siblings of Chief Louie's; they represented the *Tl'ogot'ine* (though not exclusively or in its entirety). Other village families planned to go but withdrew before the journey. Some said that salmon fishing on the Stikine was more important; pilots' weight restrictions for gear discouraged others; still others said they did not want reminders of the past. Those families that did not travel to *Hok'ats Łuwe Menh* had connections to Walker and to guiding but chose not to participate. Many non-participants were *Tl'abānot'ine*; their ancestral lands are south of the park.

Chief Louie's labelling also excludes Tahltans from *Tlēgōhīn*. This is politically astute too. Use of the term *Tl'ogot'ine* explicitly acknowledges affiliation with an Iskut past on the Spatsizi and points further east. As such, it creates distance implicitly from *Tlēgōhīn*.[8] And no Tahltan-speaking families from *Tlēgōhīn* attended the event, despite their own history of working for Walker. *Tl'ogot'ine*, then, is an obscure reference to a specific and unique history, and as such it is overtly inclusive of some Tahltan families and subtly exclusive of most others. More than this, Chief Louie's statement has the effect of reclaiming the park on the basis of an established, documented, and identifiable historical group. Such history has weight in government and legal circles. Chief Louie's opening statements present a unified, dignified, and historically demonstrable front.

Next, the chief comments on the importance of the Spatsizi Plateau as a homeland for the *Tl'ogot'ine*. The central audiences here are Iskut and non-Iskut. The speaker moves swiftly to refute Walker's assertions of ownership or control of the plateau by virtue of his guiding licence and outfit (lines 13–14). In this context, Walker himself is an audience for the speech, despite having died in 1989. Chief Louie's words about him and his role in displacing Iskut families from the area are a revision of Walker's published history (Walker 1976). The chief then takes the audience back further by citing archaeological evidence – obsidian and arrowheads – of past human activity. The implication of course is that his ancestors crafted these stone tools, and therefore Walker could not have been in the area first. Occupancy prior to arrival of Europeans forms the basis of the Iskut's claim to those lands.[9]

Chief Louie directs much of the second half of his address (from line 51 on) at contemporary political concerns. He mentions a comment that he received that morning from a 'colleague' (line 51) who insisted that 'the Tahltan have no connection to this land' (line 54). This is dangerous talk in the era of BC land claims because it hints that all Tahltan-speakers, including those at Iskut, have been away from the Spatsizi for so long that the territorial basis for their 'national' interests lacks foundation (Smith 1981, 69). Chief Louie may have directed the line also at Jenness's ethnography of the Sekanis, in which he writes that the *Tl'ogot'ine* were latecomers to the Spatsizi and had in fact usurped *Tl'abānot'ine* territory from original Tahltan speakers (Jenness 1937, 13; Sheppard 1983b, 335; also Lanoue 1992). Chief Louie refutes the comment (line 55) and thereby distances Iskut people further from undifferentiated Tahltans. He continues, building a larger case against the notion that *Tl'ogot'ine* people have no standing in the Spatsizi. He rejects the idea that Walker was ever the first settler (lines 70–71) and, in saying so, destroys the credibility of any claim that Walker might have made to local management rights on the basis of first occupancy. He reminds listeners that creation of the park was simply a case of political favouritism (line 63).

Invoking the names of elders – people with a connection to this place and to the past – is central to Chief Louie's political strategy. He does this twice. Early in the speech, he mentions a handful of people who worked extensively for Walker (lines 40–50). At this point the wind picks up, and much of the speech is inaudible to those listening. The words are unclear on the tape. Several people commented later that deceased elders were acknowledging Chief Louie's words in the gusts of wind. Iskut families were remembering these ancestors and had returned to the place where they had lived and worked largely for that purpose. Their speeches said as much.

It is unclear how the non-Iskut guests interpreted the speech or the weekend. A few attended because of long friendships with Iskut people or connections to the area. These people knew the history of this place and the weight of Chief Louie's words. While talking with other guests, however, several visitors asked me when the Iskut elders were going to tell their 'old stories' as the invitations promised. They told me that they expected an 'authentic' Native and cultural experience and that the fiddle playing, stick games, and breakfasts of bacon and eggs had disappointed them. Even though elders did not tell any myth-time stories, narratives of hunting experiences and guiding history abounded in talk at the fire or in the cook cabin. I noticed these accounts, but many other visitors did not. The weekend's events were inconsistent with their views of Aboriginality. Note here a dual perspective on Aboriginality: Native people should have stories to tell that sound like myths, and because the narratives they did tell did not sound right, they were not valid renditions of culture history.

This is the old paradox in British Columbia that I mentioned in the introduction. In his *Delgamuukw* ruling, Justice McEachern denied the legitimacy of 'old' Aboriginal stories because they were hearsay or did not sound quite right, despite their overwhelming numbers and consistency. On the Spatsizi Plateau, visitors expected to hear such accounts but heard none. Considerations of context and audience are critical for understanding the ways in which many other Canadians see Natives (see *Delgamuukw v. The Queen*, 1991; Culhane 1998). Nothing ever satisfies them.

Ultimately, this speech by Chief Louie is the most transparent account of Iskut guiding history and the emotional attachment of Iskut people to the Spatsizi that I have ever heard. The chief does not mince words: he names people and identifies places. We may attribute the tone of his speech to the outsiders present at the gathering. They needed details to make sense of his account and of the talk during the weekend. Their presence may also explain the scarcity of indexical, or synecdochal, talk about myth-time here than in other instances of historical talk. Chief Louie's frankness contrasts noticeably with the vague or non-existent contextual information in contemporary stories that Iskut people share. The non-Natives in this audience needed information to grasp the subtleties and complexities of opaque historical accounts. Chief Louie wanted everyone to understand why a return to *Hok'ats Łuwe Menh* is so important. All Iskut narrators make these kinds of rhetorical choices.

Contemporary Connections

Chief Louie's speech is more than just a revision of official history before a sympathetic audience. It represents a reaction to the economic imperialism – the search for furs and trophies in northern British Columbia and its consequences for Native lives and cultures – by earlier generations of non-Native business people (Sheppard 1983b; also Loo 2001a, b; 2006). It is a reaction to the increasing lack of control over local lands and resources Iskut people and their leaders have increasingly experienced since Walker's arrival. Of particular interest is the alienation that Iskut people feel from a homeland that is now a park. Chief Louie notes at the outset that Iskut families have been absent from the plateau for forty years (lines 4–5). This places the start of the alienation at the time of the creation of Iskut Village in the early 1960s. Tommy Walker lobbied the BC government to create the Spatsizi Plateau Wilderness Park during the early 1970s. Now, much of the area is within a provincial wilderness area that BC Parks manages. It remains Walker's legacy in northern British Columbia (Careless 1997; Henderson 2006; Loo 2006, 193–201). The official designation ended road construction and other development on the plateau. It has not eliminated Iskut hunting there entirely, and Iskut guides continue to lead non-Native hunters into the region. Regardless, many Iskut people do not like the park status. They believe that it has increased government management and bureaucracy in what they claim as their traditional lands. The Iskut leadership is working closely with BC Parks to administer these lands in ways that do not prevent hunting. Still there are perceptions by Iskut people of meddling by outsiders here, and parks are symbolic of the challenges that the wider world poses for Iskut people (also Cruikshank 2005, 66).

More generally, Chief Louie's speech makes direct and implied connections – indexes if you will – between the guiding era and the present. In the guiding era, newcomers such as Walker established businesses without showing much concern for people in the area. Today, resource companies searching for methane gas and gold present similar challenges. The chief draws the two eras together. He acknowledges, for example, the importance of Natives working with non-Native people: 'And [our future generations] are going to be in partnership with various groups of people in here, / so that we will always be connected to this great land' (lines 26–27).

But much of the connection that he draws between past and present is more subtle; it emerges through metaphor and allusion. It relies on the image of Walker and implies that care, as well as accommodation, is critical to successful management of local lands. Chief Louie makes this point by talking about the past as an example of events that should not occur again when he notes that 'Walker had a lot of influence in Victoria' in the mid-1950s (line 63). Now Iskut leaders control the northern economy, even if park boundaries complicate their ability to live or work on the Spatsizi Plateau. The Collingwoods placated the Iskut First Nation by organizing this event. The government officials present learned something of the oral history of the people in this part of the province.

Historian Tina Loo's perspective on Walker and his legacy in northern British Columbia differs significantly from that of Iskut leaders such as Chief Louie (Loo 2006). Focusing on Walker's personality and his reasons for wanting to see protection of the Spatsizi as a wilderness park, Loo indicates that Walker drew moral connections between wilderness and the Tahltan-speaking people within it (2006, 209). Walker seems to have genuinely wanted to protect the Spatsizi for the betterment of the Tahltans and all Canadians. Writes Loo: 'For [Walker], the value of wild places went far beyond recreation or aesthetics. Instead, Spatsizi . . . Country [was] significant for broader social reasons. Wilderness cultivated different ways of being in people – fellowship, connection, humility – and for that reason it was worth protecting. From [his] vantage point in the back country, Walker . . . could see the link between environmental integrity and social integrity. For [him], protecting wild places was the key to upholding a way of life – for people as well as for animals' (209).

Loo suggests that Walker valued greatly his relationships with Aboriginal people in part because 'he did not hold the local white population in high esteem, considering it boorish' (195). But she also points out that Walker couched this esteem in the rhetoric of the noble savage (195, quoting Walker 1976, 55) and invoked the notion that Tahltan people lived close to nature as Walker himself preferred and in a way that might benefit all Canadians. According to Loo, Walker chose to live at

Hok'ats Łuwe Menh because of his sensibilities towards a wilderness that he contrasted with his urban youth. But when Iskut people talk about Walker they express mixed feelings, partly because his efforts to *create* wilderness are antithetical to the Iskut experiences in that same place. Iskut people do not talk in terms of modernity. They do not character-ize their connections to the Spatsizi in terms of a choice to live close to nature. For them, the Spatsizi is neither wild nor unknown. Iskut people do not remember it in contrast to somewhere else; rather, the Spatsizi is home.

Transcript 5.2: *Deneka'ladiyah* Story on BC Parks Sign Board

One other episode at the *Hok'ats Łuwe Menh* reunion camp is relevant here. It involves outsiders' expectations about Iskut hunting talk. I encountered a version of the *Deneka'ladiyah* story on a sign leaning against the wall in Tommy Walker's old guiding-era workshop. This is the story of the hunter who disrespected a goat and was turned to stone for his foolish actions (see above, chapter 4). The tale takes place in the Spatsizi, and a rock formation along the Spatsizi River marks the hunter's transformation. The Iskut band office produced the text – a very brief version of the tale that Iskut elder Sophia Stanton told me and that Teit recorded (1919, 248–50).

The new *Deneka'ladiyah* story at *Hok'ats Łuwe Menh* is as follows:

> Denkladia (Den kha-la-dia), 'Man Walking With Spear': 'There was once a goat that a man could not kill. He was a tough goat. The man said to him, "I'm going to follow you 'til you go back home to your dad," meaning that the hunter was not about to give up so easily. Then, just as he was spearing the goat he said, "*Thehe on dine*." This means, "Change into rock." And the goat, the man and his dog all turned into rock.'

Analysis

This version of *Deneka'ladiyah* begins with the confrontation between a hunter and a goat that is too cunning to be killed. While this kind of encounter is common in Iskut hunting talk, human relations with animals have changed, and the hunter is now more powerful than the animal. The hunter's comments imply that he will continue to hunt the goat until it returns to its father's house, potentially a safe place. In

Sophia Stanton's and Teit's versions of the story, the hunter scolds the goat for not offering itself up to the persistent hunter; his own punishment stems from his speaking improperly to the animal. The difference between the versions is subtle but significant. In the new version, the choice of the goat to sacrifice itself evaporates because the hunter will not give up his pursuit. Still, the outcome is the same in all versions of the story. Presumably, the lesson not to talk badly about animals is the same, too.

What strikes me most about this version is the power that it affords to the hunter who refuses to leave the goat alone. He states explicitly that he will not give up. This is different from the stance of hunters in most hunting talk and _sa'e_ stories who find that they are subject to the power of animals. Remember, Arthur Nole and Colin Duncan both express disgust at their inability to kill a moose but nevertheless let the animal go (chapter 3). While I understand that this version might have been shortened to fit it on the sign, there is a contemporary twist here: hunters have become more powerful over time and now have the upper hand in their relations with prey. Could the message here be that after generations of benevolent animals providing for them, Iskut people must now start caring for the animals? Has the sacrificial imagery inverted completely? The arrests of Iskut elders in 2005 for blocking access to developers to the hunting grounds suggest in fact that some Iskut people are willing now to sacrifice themselves for the animals and the land on which they live.

The sign is more for visitors to the wilderness park than for Iskut audiences. Perhaps the sign's creators meant to add some Aboriginal colour to the camp and to authenticate the Native experience for hikers from Vancouver or Seattle. For such adventurers, the story is an expression of Iskut identity and local history – elements of being _didene_ – in a form that sounds like a myth. It describes a seemingly fantastic event, the transformation of a man, dog, and goat into rock, and it is visible to non-Natives. Park visitors, like the guests at the reunion camp, might expect to encounter this kind of Native lore, since the website for the park acknowledges Native connections to the place.

More than this, the sign's story is a shared narrative at Iskut. All Iskut families claim it, tell it, and refer to it legitimately. It is not a family history or a narrative of an individual's hunting experience. For these reasons, community leaders can use the _Deneka'ladiyah_ story as one element of the Iskut hunting legacy. The sign also epitomizes the tendency of Iskut storytellers to share contracted, shortened versions of old stories when the audience – whether it consists of Iskut children, anthropologists, or government representatives – knows little about local history and culture. This version of the tale provides further evidence that Iskut people use their hunting legacy strategically – for reasons of affiliation and distancing – in new and 'multicultural' settings (also Dinwoodie 2002, 64).

Both Chief Louie's speech and the BC Parks sign serve as reminders of the hunting prowess of Iskut people. They are examples of the way in which the Iskut express themselves when non-Natives are listening closely. The speech presents Iskut history and hunting activities more directly than most other hunting talk I heard. In delivering it, Chief Louie acknowledges the audience and the relationships that Iskut people have with outsiders and how they have changed for recent generations. The address is consistent, in fact, with Iskut relationships with non-Native people back in time to the guiding era. And it acknowledges the complexity of interpersonal relations between Iskut people, past and present. The sign downplays the control that animals have over people. It indicates that social connections between hunters and their prey have changed and Iskut people have greater power. Intriguingly today, Iskut people desire greater control in local politics and resource economics. Again, the audience is critical. Hikers reaching the centre of the Spatsizi Plateau can add a touch of Native lore to their experience. For Iskut people, it is a minor expression of ethnicity. It offers a subtle, yet poignant, affirmation of Iskut history and presence in the area. Both the speech and the board are crafted – and crafty – presentations of Iskut hunting heritage and knowledge. They present local issues in terms that non-Native people expect and understand.

6 Everyday Talk about Hunting

Today I hear lots of these young guys say, 'We going hunting,' and they take four-wheeler vehicle. Not our style. Walk. Track 'em down. That's what we do. Sure.

—Iskut Elder Arthur Nole at the Klappan
Independent Day School, 2002

A central observation stemming from my ethnographic analysis of Iskut hunting talk is the tendency of speakers to cover, or obscure, their hunting heritage with artistic speech. This occurs when the stigma of hunting as an impoverished economy, or Iskut culture as an impoverished culture, enters a conversation (Goffman 1963, 102). The fact that Iskut people 'cover' hunting talk suggests that they are uncomfortable talking about it in some situations. More significant, it indicates that they make conscious choices about what to say, and to whom, about their sustenance activities. These observations of mine are hardly surprising. They are noteworthy, however, because the choice to cover or not results from the historical circumstances in which Iskut people learned that not everyone saw hunting as a reputable way to live. This stigma has developed during interactions with outsiders. It is evident in the books that outsiders have written about poor Indians (e.g., Walker 1976). Studies of traditional use and traditional ecological knowledge (TEK) perpetuate it when they attempt to encode Native knowledge in non-Native and scientific formats; Natives are not experts, after all. It continues when outsiders ask why Native people receive 'special treatment,' such as tax breaks and free housing on reserves. This is the politics of being *didene* and, by extension, the politics of hunting as expressed in hunting talk. Such talk – should you care to listen – reflects Iskut reactions to the contest for resources, animals, and minerals that have preoccupied people in northwestern British Columbia for eons.

At times, Iskut hunters cover their actions when talking with other Native hunters. They may do so to downplay differences in family histories. Covering also allows hunters to talk about their exploits without speaking disrespectfully about their prey. It helps hunters not show off. The fact that covering is so common is another reminder that hunting talk is rarely explicit. Only close readings of texts and contexts can uncover and interpret connections between hunting, history, and everyday life.

Talk and actions that sound like 'affiliation' with a hunting past balance the covering of that past with prideful association. Affiliation is important in political circumstances or during negotiations with resource companies. In these moments, outsiders demand such talk. Knowledge of lands, animals, and resources – talking TEK – identifies Iskut people as Aboriginal. In turn, that talk increasingly validates Iskut rights to lands and resources in the minds of observers who do not know much else about Iskut history. In sum, covering and affiliation talk are used by Iskut speakers of all ages to exert control over their own interpersonal relationships and their own exploitation of the land and animals. The problem is that outsiders do not usually hear such statements as an assertion of control.

However I express it, I understand that Iskut people share a common interest in hunting and its practices. The meaning of hunting at Iskut Village exists in verbal expressions that identify a connection to the past and create an identity in the present. Hunting persists because it serves as a moral anchor for individual behaviour. Because Iskut people frequently measure individual character with reference to hunting, I believe that they would continue to hunt even in the absence of the cash economy that supports hunting for food. Hunting unites people, places, and animals with the rules by which people must behave, and it gives people a venue for confronting changes to those rules. This plays out when individuals make choices about shooting moose or leaving them alone. It appears in the variety of ways in which villagers respond to the activities of outsiders. We can see it when Iskut people cover their hunting activities or myth-time knowledge.

I have presented specific examples of the place of hunting in the lives of Iskut people. My focus has been on the way in which people talk about hunting in everyday and non-bureaucratic settings, and I have set this talk into detailed ethnographic descriptions of how hunting occurs in Iskut today. Moreover, I have positioned the hunting talk against a general observation that outsiders have not always appreciated Iskut culture, and hunting in particular, as a fully contemporary activity. This has prompted me throughout the text to describe or imply a number of parallels and paradoxes in Iskut relations with other people. Iskut people recognize ties with other Tahltan-speaking peoples, but only to a point. Shared language and cultural features unite all Tahltans at weddings, at funerals, during salmon fishing on the Stikine River, and when large numbers of people (or demonstration of a large and contiguous land base) prove essential for political action. Divisions exist within this large Tahltan group over guiding history, territorial claims, and management of lands and resources.

Iskut relationships with non-Natives are equally complicated. Tommy Walker epitomizes the ire that many people at Iskut feel towards meddling outsiders who do not fully understand the complexities of living lives as hunters. Yet he brought with him opportunities that residents embraced quickly and easily. He brought a business into the area that provided Iskut people with clear roles and considerable control. The same is true today when anthropologists (such as I) express an interest in traditional uses of local lands or mining companies seek (without always finding) village support for economic development. The greater web of life at Iskut – predicated on social relationships with sentient animals – also exemplifies many of these challenges. The spiritual aspects of sustenance hunting appear to conflict with the pragmatism of wage-based hunting and guiding. Residents treat food animals differently from domesticated ones. Yet Iskut people have enthusiastically embraced both activities and the animals associated with them.

Hunting, then, is a shared set of practices encoded in narratives. It is central to a cultural system at Iskut Village where only some history unites people within the place. This system relies on shared symbols that reflect both contemporary practices and longstanding traditions. Conversational narratives contain these symbols, which point to the management of personal and social identities. In other words, Iskut people express and demonstrate their concern for the group and for social relations within the group with talk of hunting. Likewise, the talk disseminates local values about the sharing of food, social relations with animals, or threats from outsiders.

Ethnography and TEK

The frequent discussion of Iskut's hunting history by Iskut people is telling. It reflects historical realities such as their long-term interactions with outsiders. It points to how savvy they have become at describing their rights, history, and traditions in an increasingly litigious and confrontational relationship with governments and developers. The casual sharing of guiding stories between *pāne*, 'partner,' conveys the same disgust with Tommy Walker as a chief's speech in front of government representatives. The presentations are, however, different. The audiences are, of course, different. In the conversation, the speakers share guiding history subtly and allude to the past indirectly. In the address, the chief reshapes guiding history as a specific and continuing threat to local sovereignty while people in government look on. Varying histories, family origins, and hunting experiences do not mean that a cultural identity is lacking. Rather, cultural coherence and logic emerge around hunting, guiding, and work with outsiders.

Significantly, the rules and processes of hunting described here are most visible outside of formal interviews and myth-time stories. Conversational narratives about hunting are rife with information about hunting practices, animal behaviour, hunting etiquette, and the importance of knowing local lands. This is traditional ecological knowledge, if one wants to see it that way. But these conversations, these stories, show the dynamic and varied applications of such knowledge in everyday Iskut lives. *Sa'e* stories have not disappeared entirely, and they contribute to assertions of ethnic nationhood, particularly when recorded in interviews with James Teit or me. It is unclear, however, if these narratives reinforce an Iskut identity locally or a Tahltan identity regionally. Often the non-Native researcher saying *something* about Native naturalness does not care to distinguish between these two identities, which seek purchase and, at times, find display in Iskut. Now, *sa'e* stories are less frequent vehicles for transmitting local truths about animals and history. Other narratives have taken their place.

Like Iskut people themselves, I am keen to find the best ways to document, record, and represent Native relationships with local lands and food supplies. Originally, I thought Traditional Use Studies (TUSs) were inauthentic or incomplete representations of local knowledge. In some ways, they are precisely that, and I still find the absence of individual voices in such studies frustrating. It is very hard to quantify hunting talk or to put it on maps, despite its vitality, richness, and distinctive character. I have also worried that TEK and TUSs in bureaucratic settings idealize Native people as close to nature and perhaps primitive. These criticisms are not entirely fair. A TUS may be a foreign format for documenting local knowledge. Iskut people have, however, learned it, become adept at using it, and made it as much part of their repertoire for demonstrating their history and rights as any rhetorical or narrative strategy. My complaint is that researchers undertake TUSs and apply TEK in research settings where other techniques, including the ethnography of speaking, or the documentation of stories, might be more appropriate or useful. TUSs and TEK work have a place, but they should not replace other ways of documenting Aboriginal knowledge of lands and animals. I am advocating here for nothing more than an acceptance of the fact that Iskut Villagers employ a range of responses to outsiders, development projects, or court decisions in their regular performances of sovereignty and dignity.

At Iskut, the stories of the past told openly in the present are reminders of a long and substantial association with sustenance hunting. The material importance of hunted meat pales next to its symbolic and social significance. Attending to everyday forms of speech can illuminate the differences between affiliation and covering, materialism and symbolism, and demonstrate the utility of hunting talk in a Native community today. Situations that minimize this history point to the stigma of living as hunters in an industrial world. The value of hunting stories for Iskut people stems from their utility in a range of situations. They indicate how personal relations with animals are changing. Telling them helps Iskut people address, engage, and manage their footing in a wider world that is often rife with interpersonal tensions, litigious actions, racism, and concerns about the land.

New Challenges Highlight the Politics of Hunting

Engaging with outsiders continues to present opportunities and challenges for Iskut people. Since 2005, they and their Tahltan-speaking relatives at *Tlēgōhīn* have participated in a number of civil actions in defence of local management of land and resources (see Paulson 2006). These actions imply that defining or protecting or performing local sovereignty is not just the prerogative of elected leaders. In Iskut Village, negotiations with resource companies over mineral and timber rights have dominated local politics in recent years. Specifically, there are coal and coalbed methane (natural gas) fields in the *Tl'abāne*, headwaters of *Hok'āz*

Tū'e; Arthur Nole's *Didini Kime* is there, and it sits on a mountain of coal. The area is known increasingly as the Sacred Headwaters in deference to the sources of the Nass, Skeena, and Stikine Rivers, which all sit within a few kilometres of each other. The Iskut people initially responded to impending development of this area by Fortune Minerals and Shell Canada by considering acquiring their own drilling platform and keeping the resource royalties for themselves (Louis Louie, personal communication). That idea was short-lived. After thinking about the damage to hunting grounds that mining might bring, the Iskut First Nation formally asked Shell Canada to leave its territory in the spring of 2005.

In the summer and autumn of 2005, Iskut people, mainly women, blocked the road to the coal and methane gas fields to traffic from non-Native mining companies (see Carmichael 2005).[1] For two months, the protesters positioned themselves at the beginning of the long, dusty road into the *Tl'abāne* and denied trucks access to the area. Then, in September 2005, a judge issued an injunction against them. The mining company prepared to move its trucks up the grade. The protesters donned black-and-red button blankets, usually symbols of coastal Native groups, and refused to leave. The Royal Canadian Mounted Police arrested thirteen Iskut people, including nine elders. Neo-liberal resource politics, supported by the actions of the courts and police, quashed local agency. In an Iskut idiom, the arrests were a sacrifice on behalf of animals.

I followed these events from Vancouver. E-mail and phone calls with people who visited the blockade kept me up to date. I also consulted Internet-based media, including news-gathering websites and a blog by Iskut authors. The blog distributed photographs and news stories from the Canadian Press. It also provided general information about the condition of the protesters, the status of the blockade, and the goals of the protest. One blog entry described these goals this way: 'Blockaders are stopping access to the Mount Klappan and the Sacred Headwaters, where the first trickles of four magnificent rivers flow – Spatsizi, Nass, Klappan, and Skeena. The surrounding Stikine is a globally significant natural area and the centre of Tahltan culture. The salmon from these rivers and the wildlife and plants have sustained Tahltan for thousands of years' (3 September 2005; www.tahltan.blogspot.com, accessed 20 September 2005). Local civil disobedience is couched in global terms.

These events, I perceive, are consistent with the struggles of indigenous peoples against resource developers in other parts of British Columbia, Canada, and around the world. They follow Dene resistance to the MacKenzie Valley Pipeline during the 1970s, where the Dene feared that the environmental impact of the pipeline would cause harm to traditional foraging practices (Asch 1982, 351). Asch observes that Dene acculturation in the context of that development was not inevitable, although slowing or preventing acculturation required accommodating Dene interests (353). Similar examples exist elsewhere in Canada and around the world. Quebec Crees faced, and protested, the impacts of the Great Whale hydroelectric development, also during the 1970s (Feit 2010, 66). While today Crees recognize the need for resource development because it can support their interests too, Feit reminds readers that such support requires respectful dialogue and negotiated land-use agreements. He continues, noting that respect and negotiation has not always worked in ways that reflect traditional outlooks: 'Giving up on [co-governance] agreements to solely emphasize cosmopolitan or oppositional social movements would diminish Crees, for it would devalue their visions, practices, and historical experiences. It would shift their struggle for survival more to the terrain of neoliberal governmentalities and their cosmopolitan assumptions. This is not the case for all Indigenous struggles, but it is one of the ways many Crees seek to live and survive in a world shaped significantly by both Crees and non-Crees' (Feit 2010, 77–78).

Continuing, Iskut resistance to mining appears similar to the Clayoquot Sound protests (Magnusson and Shaw 2003) and the struggles of Nuxalk elders (Pynn 2000) – both on the BC coast in the early to mid-1990s – to turn loggers away from traditional food-gathering and spiritual places. The protests connect implicitly to the land and Aboriginal-title disputes of the Tsilhqot'in of British Columbia (*Tsilhqot'in Nation v. British Columbia* 2007). And, the fight of Iskut hunters against industries they see as harmful to their hunting territories and, ultimately, their way of life is reminiscent of logging and mining protests in Papua New Guinea (Barker 2007). Acculturation to neoliberal programs may not be inevitable but preventing it from happening takes work that frequently brings indigenous peoples into conflict with the laws and expectations of the state.

The struggles between indigenous peoples and industrialists are never simple. Just like the groups that make up contemporary Aboriginal villages, these fights involve multiple parties and opinions. The Iskut arrests of 2005 divided families along gender and generational lines. They created rifts between elected leaders and traditional family-based and matrilineal leaders. They reminded me once again that a shared village is rarely enough to obscure the divisions that endure along family or regional lines. The most visible people on the blockade were women, and many of them had spoken at *Hok'ats Łuwe Menh* a year earlier. The wife of the elected chief was arrested, along with four of his sisters (Carmichael 2005). At first, the Iskut leadership publicly denounced the blockade, citing the need for mining-related jobs. The protesters countered with claims about the importance of sustainable management of resources; they easily mastered the language of resource development. Later, the elected leaders came out against some of the exploration and development. Charges against arrested protesters were stayed on Hallowe'en 2005.

Despite the visible fractures along the lines of leadership, the protests against methane-gas exploration united families across their ancestral divisions. Through 2005 and into 2006 and 2007, descendants of the *Tl'abānot'ine* and the *Tl'ogot'ine* worked together to protect the ancestral homes of both groups. Protesters erected more blockades (Figure 8). Lilian Moyer, a Tahltan elder, was arrested in 2006. The intriguing use of ethnonyms was on display at the blockades. In August 2006, for example, one Iskut elder proclaimed publicly his rejection of the label 'Tahltan,' preferring instead *Tl'abānot'ine* as a marker of personal identification and affiliation. I overheard him make the comment when a representative of the Tahltan Central Council (TCC), which represents the Tahltan and the Iskut First Nations in resource negotiations, visited the blockade. The representative tried to walk a fine line between supporting the protesters and furthering the belief that some mining was central to the economic interests of the regional government. The elder asserted his dislike for the political manoeuvring and the meddling of an outsider – a Tahltan person but not an Iskut, *Tl'abānot'ine*, or *Tl'ogot'ine* person – by his strategic use of ethnonyms.

The current mining proposals do not cross the Spatsizi Plateau Wilderness Park boundary. Instead, they run conspicuously along the southwestern boundary of the park, where most Iskut hunting occurs and where road access already exists. Is the park's protection of the hunting grounds of the *Tl'ogot'ine* from mining to be the final legacy of Tommy Walker? The park has, after all, pushed mining development into the traditional lands of the *Tl'abānot'ine*, the historical neighbours of the *Tl'ogot'ine*, and into the lands that all Iskut people use extensively and share today.

Iskut people have confronted, and variously embraced or rejected, the intrusions of outsiders and their mercantile and capitalist activities. There has not been a standard response to guide outfitters or railroad

Iskut blockade against Shell Canada, 2007. This photograph (used with permission) was taken by Frances Marion, a young Tahltan person. The picture is remarkable: it clearly juxtaposes the line of Aboriginal protesters, including a woman wearing a button blanket and holding a drum, with the representative of Shell, wearing a cowboy hat and cowboy boots and reading the court injunction against the blockade. RCMP officers look on.

builders or miners – other than that narratives of acceptance and conflict are widely shared (also Feit 2010, 51). Still, patterns emerge. Guiding appears palatable because it requires Iskut people and their skills as hunters. The sparring between Iskut people and outsiders that exists in a guiding context is associated with the personalities of the outfitters, like Walker; the work itself, while hard, is remembered fondly. Iskut people remember fondly the central roles they played in the industry. In contrast, recent mineral exploration has tested the patience of most Iskut people (also Morgan 2009). My sense from listening to Iskut people talk about mining is that they feel that their voice, nay their experience, is not considered seriously in the decisions being made about the lands they call home. Control has become elusive.

By attending to the stories of northern development, hunting, and history from Iskut, Native perspectives can help us understand the benefits and shortcomings of neo-liberal policies and global processes.[2] Blaser et al. insist that globalization is reconfiguring the web of life in indigenous communities (2010, 9). At Iskut, as in other northern hunting societies, the web of life draws people from disparate backgrounds together in novel combinations. Moreover, it continues to unite people, animals, and the land in ways that demonstrate that animals are people and the land is animated by relationships of understanding, care, confrontation, and respect. Current conflicts are tightening, not breaking, the bonds among those resisting global change. Arthur's and Colin's hunting stories reiterate these relationships in mythological terms. Robert's guiding stories illustrate both the conflict and enjoyment that came from working for bosses and client hunters, who do not actually appear directly in the stories. The directness of Chief Louie's speech underlines the changes that have taken place in the past generation; miners, and the activities they pursue, are not incorporated into the local web of life and its demands of reciprocity in the way that earlier explorers and hunters were (Feit 2004, 102). In short, industrial developers do not understand that Iskut people are not always motivated by royalties or jobs. An active role in the management of the land and animals – one that does not demand a separation of nature from culture – is more important.[3]

Resistance to mining by many Iskut people will continue in the form of speeches and protests, I expect, until respect for the land is balanced with the sacrifice the land might make of its minerals. While there are no obvious mythological charters for blockades, Chief Louie's speech and the narrative renditions of hunting memories remind me that Iskut people frequently refashion old ideas about respect in novel ways. The rhetoric at the blockades and conversations at *Hok'ats Łuwe Menh* remind other people to treat land, like food animals, properly, or it will cease to provide the materials of life. Exploiting the land like a work animal is untenable and foolhardy. Chief Louie tells us that the guiding era and Iskut associations with Tommy Walker are a useful charter for behaviour when outsiders are around. And his words indicate that Iskut people are quick to embrace change when it is beneficial and will reflect on those changes as time passes.[4] That is part of being *didene*. I expect that we will hear stories of the latest intrusions into Iskut territory by mining companies – the new Tommy Walkers, if you like – in the years to come.

Appendix

Tahltan-Language Place Names

Place Name	English Common Name	Literal English Translation and Other Notes
Dane'hih	Donahue Pass	Donahue (Danahue) Pass near *Hok'ats Łuwe Menh*. The valley named for a person named *Dane'hih*.
Deneka'ladiyah	No English equivalent is used.	'Person who walked into a spear'; *Deneka'ladiyah* consists of several morphemes. *Dene* means person. The word for spear/arrowhead is *ka'*, and *la* is tip of the arrow. *Diyah* means he/she walked or ran into it (Angela Dennis, personal communication).
Didini Tū'e	Didene Creek	Young caribou creek; *didini* means 'young caribou' (the similarly-sounding word '*didene*' means 'Native person'), and *tū'e* is creek.
Dzełtsedle	Klappan Mountain	Little mountain; *dzeł* is mountain and *tsedle* is small or little. Some people call this mountain *Tsētsedle*.
Edōnetenajān Menh	Eddontenajon Lake	'Child under water'; *Edōnetenajān* consists of several morphemes. *Edōne* is child, although the story tells of a boy. *Tenh tl'ā* means under water (Carter, Carlick, and Carlick 1994, 212), and it appears contracted to simply *ten(h)* in the name. *Tl'ā* may be represented by *ajā* in current usage, although this is speculation on my part. Indeed, it seems possible that at one time the name, perhaps prior to anglicization, *Edōnetenajān* was *Edōne-tenh- tl'ā(n)*.

(*continued*)

Tahltan-Language Place Names (*continued*)

Place Name	English Common Name	Literal English Translation and Other Notes
Hok'ats Łuwe Menh	Cold Fish Lake	Cold fish lake; *hok'ats* is cold, *łuwe* is fish, and *menh* is lake.
Hok'āz Tū'e	(Big) Klappan River	Filing river; *hok'āz* is filing and *tū'e* is river. In other words, the river files through its banks as it shapes its valley.
Kāti Chō	No English equivalent is used by Iskut people; it is spelled locally as Kawdy Chō.	Big slide; named for a large rock slide area nearby. *Kāti* is slide, and *chō* is big.
Kenes̱'kani Menh	Kinaskan Lake	Raft across; kenes̱ means raft; kani is, presumably, a directional related to movement across.
Łuwechōn Menh	Kluachon Lake; also Iskut Lake	Big fish; *łuwe* is fish, and *chō(n)* is big. Known colloquially as Skoot Lake.
Me'etsendāne	Metsantan	Always full stomachs; a reference to the quantities of food in the area
Mo'uchōhe Menh	Morchuea Lake	Translation unknown; may mean big lake where Mo means *menh*, 'lake,' and *chō* is 'big.' I also heard that the name refers to the big fish that are found in the lake.
S̱etū	Zetu Creek	Mountain water; s̱e is a contraction of *ts̱ē* (mountain), and *tū* is water.
Spatsizi	Spatsizi	This place name is in common English usage. It is a contraction of *is̱bā*, meaning goat, and *detsī dzi*, meaning red.
Stikine	Stikine; possibly of Tlingit origin.	The *Tahltan Children's Illustrated Dictionary* (Carter, Carlick, and Carlick 1994, 125) says that *Tūdes̱e,* 'river,' is also used for the Stikine. I never heard anyone use *Tūdes̱e* in place of Stikine.
Tatāge Menh	Tatogga Lake	Water in between; refers to the position of *Tatāge Menh* between other, larger lakes.
Tatl'ah	Dease Lake	Headwaters; Dease Lake is the headwater lake for the Dease River, which flows into the Arctic Ocean
Tl'abāne	Klappan; also written as Klabona	Open grass flats; refers to the plateau area where the headwaters of the *Tl'abāne Tū'e* are located.

Place Name	English Common Name	Literal English Translation and Other Notes
Tl'abāne Tū'e	Little Klappan River	Open grass flats river.
Tlēgōhīn	Telegraph Creek	Raspberry creek; the name is of Tlingit origin (Carter, Carlick, and Carlick 1994, 126).
Tsēghādetsen'	Stingy Mountain	Stingy mountain; *eghādetsen'* is stingy, and *tsē* is mountain.
Tsētsedle	Klappan Mountain	Little mountain or little rock; *tsē* is mountain or rock, and *tsedle* is small or little. Some people call this mountain *Dzeɬtsedle*.
Tuhtseyghuda'	Loon Beak	Loon beak; *tuhtsey* is loon, and -*da'* is beak (Carter, Carlick, and Carlick 1994, 152).

Notes

Introduction

1 Throughout the book, I present the Tahltan-language place names I heard in use in the Tahltan practical orthography. See Appendix, Tahltan-Language Place Names, for the English gloss or English common name of place names as well as literal translations.

2 Arthur Nole's name is not a pseudonym. All names in this book are pseudonyms unless the person is a historical figure or otherwise noted.

3 A short note on terminology: Because of the variable and fluid nature of a Tahltan identity, I avoid using 'Tahltan' as an unmodified noun or as a non-specific adjective unless the context is clear. I use 'First Nation' only in political contexts or when a proper noun, such as 'Iskut,' requires it. The word 'band' is a legal term in Canada referring to a group of registered Indians (yet another legal term) under the Indian Act. Some Iskut people, particularly those who work in the band office, use the word 'band' to refer to the collective group living at Iskut Village. I prefer the word 'Native' or 'Aboriginal' for indigenous BC people, and these are standard terms of reference inside and outside Native communities. I am also careful with the term 'elders.' At Iskut, elders are culturally knowledgeable people, usually over fifty-five. They eat first at feasts and receive recognition at public events. I distinguish these people from other adults over fifty-five who are not recognized as having the knowledge of elders and from men and women under the age of fifty-five. Under an agreement with the Iskut First Nation Council, I use pseudonyms for personal names where I have not received explicit permission to use real names, but, after discussions with Council, I have not changed the names of places, geographical features, or historical figures.

4 In words in the Tahltan practical orthography, every letter is pronounced. So, *didene* is dee-den-eh.
5 Free translation: Long time ago it was harder, where people went to hunt. Today we use vehicles, but we are still Native people.
6 I use sustenance instead of subsistence in this manuscript in deference to an Iskut woman's feeling that the word subsistence implied poverty in the sense of 'barely subsisting.' She preferred sustenance because hunting, in her words, 'sustains her culture.'

1. Aboriginal Hunting in an Era of Traditional Ecological Knowledge

1 Hunting offers a useful metaphor for understanding life in many northern Athapaskan communities (e.g., Honigmann 1946:35; Brody 1988; Ridington 1988; Sharp 2001). Others have noted a similar focus on hunting in Cree communities (e.g., Tanner 1979, xii).
2 I take seriously Asch's call in 1982 to study hunting as it appears in the contemporary world and not only as an historical activity (Asch 1982, 369).
3 A Traditional Use Study is a research project designed to create maps and a database of places deemed culturally significant to an Aboriginal community. Archival research, interviews with elders, and site visits form the basis for these projects.
4 Furniss (1999, 122) and Culhane (1998, 46, note 8) use essentially the same definition of racism, and it works for my purposes, too. Furniss writes: 'racism [is] an ideology that distinguishes one group of people as being inherently different from others based on phenotypical characteristics and that assigns certain negatively evaluated characteristics, abilities, or behaviours, whether biological or cultural, as definitive of and natural for this group as a whole' (1999, 122).
5 There are numerous anthropological accounts of racism, of the history of racist beliefs, towards Native people in Canada. See, for example, Fisher 1977; Lanoue 1990, 49; Ridington 1990a; Tennant 1990; Coates 1991; Menzies 1994; Culhane 1998; Furniss 1999; Brody 2000.
6 For comparison, see Sandlos's comments about perceptions of Aboriginal hunting in the Northwest Territories (2007, 12).
7 Ethnoecology is a subset of ethnoscience (Vayda and Rappaport 1968, 489; Moran 2000, 63; also Nazarea 1999, vii; 1). Ethnoecologists seek cognitive categories within cultural groups to understand the relationships that people have with their local environments. This endeavour includes an effort to contextualize ethnoscientific observations in broader descriptions and in doing so criticizes ethnoscience for assuming that classifications are themselves statements of ethnoecology (Vayda and Rappaport 1968, 489).

8 Menzies and Butler add that TEK is cumulative knowledge that is long-term, dynamic, historical, local, holistic, moral, and spiritual in conception (Menzies and Butler 2006, 7).

9 Widdowson and Howard offer a scathing attack on the credibility and utility of TEK. They challenge the fiscal and social responsibility of the bureaucracy associated with TEK research in the context of environmental assessments and, more generally, in public policy. They assert that TEK is one component of a massive Aboriginal industry that, ultimately, prevents the integration of Aboriginal peoples into broader Canadian society (Widdowson and Howard 2008, 13). Widdowson and Howard have been criticized, too, largely because of their poor use of cultural evolutionary theory and their inflammatory language (Westman 2010).

10 Geertz (1983) uses the term 'local knowledge' differently than critics of TEK research, such as Cruikshank. Geertz says that it consists of local views of events set within local contexts (215) and focuses on the interpretation of these events. Government-sponsored TEK projects, of the sort that industrial developers undertake, do not always consider local contexts, preferring instead to lift TEK out of context in order to complete basic reporting requirements of consultation projects that emphasize unconnected places and not larger contexts. See also Loo (2001a, 116) for a consideration of Geertz's use of the phrase 'local knowledge.'

11 Academic applications of TEK frequently offer rich presentations of this kind of information (e.g., Hunn 1990; Menzies and Butler 2006). Unlike scholarly ethnoscience, however, TEK has a significant position in bureaucratic projects and reports. Paying Native organizations to document TEK is one way governments can demonstrate compliance with a ruling by the Supreme Court of Canada that governments must consult with Aboriginal peoples before resource development on traditional lands can occur (*British Columbia v. Haida Nation et al.* 2004). TEK becomes a convenient and seemingly simple tool for governments to solicit input on resource-related activities.

12 The ethnography of speaking seeks to illustrate how language unfolds in social contexts. In 1962, Hymes detailed a program for an ethnography of speaking that drew together ethnographic inquiry and linguistics research in order to use verbal behaviour in context as a means for describing human behaviour (1962, 45). This was a shift from thinking about language in the absence of culture to considering how cultural events shaped speakers' choice of words (Valentine 1995, 5). Bauman and Sherzer require that the ethnographer of speaking determine the 'resources available to members of a speech community for the conduct of speaking' (1974, 7;

cf. Gumperz 1972, 219). From here, one can identify differences in spoken behaviour within small communities.

While the ethnography of speaking suits my interest in the use of hunting talk in specific social events, it is not without its problems. Critics cite a lack of theoretical unity and a generally functionalist interest in explaining what speech acts and events do for individuals and groups as specific issues (Duranti 1997, 13, 290; Keating 2001, 294). Dinwoodie's concern for the incongruence between what people say and how they feel about the past is a critique of functionalist explanations (2002, 6).

13 In general, narratives are temporally ordered creations or elicitations (Finnegan 1992, 13; Manelis Klein 1999, 167), which – and here I am informed by Peircean semiotics (Peirce 1992) – act as verbal icons of past events (Bauman 1986, 5, cited by Crapanzano 1996, 111). Grasping the relationship between narration and narrated events is critical to understanding local meanings (Bauman 1986, 5). In my experience at Iskut, local meanings might exist as transparent icons (statements) of past events. Yet they might just as readily constitute performances of past events that use the past symbolically, metaphorically, to comment on present-day activities. The ethnography of speaking is a useful method because context is central to distinguishing and interpreting these presentations.

14 Robert Quock's name is not a pseudonym.

15 Note, however, that Arthur Nole begins the story in transcript 0.1 (introduction) with ṣa'e. While a ṣa'e story points to myth-time, it is also a conventional introduction to stories that take place in the past.

16 See Patrick Moore (2002, 41–42; 2007, 70) for comparative genres among the Kaska, neighbours of the Tahltans to the north.

17 Sheppard refers to short references to myth-time stories at Iskut as 'conversational retellings,' applying Hymes's idea that some storytellers assume responsibility for knowing the content of traditional stories but not for performances of them (Sheppard 1983a, 90; Hymes 1975, republished in Hymes 1981).

18 The meaning of the Tahltan name Nākdił is not known.

19 Valentine discusses a similar genre for Severn Ojibwe storytellers (Valentine 1995, 171). Preston notes the same for Quebec Cree (2002, 254–57).

20 Ridington's research among Dunne-za (Beaver) Athapaskans is an exception to this in British Columbia. He remarks that hunting stories are a form of technology that hunters carry with them to negotiate their use of local environments (1990c). He reports that Dunne-za hunters label tales of this sort 'wise stories' (Ridington and Ridington 2006, 97–104).

21 A community linked linguistically to the Severn Ojibwe described by Valentine (1995).

22 Feit's research with Cree speakers and storytellers demonstrates that, like Tahltans, Cree beliefs limit distinctions between animals and people (Feit 2010, 53). He also notes that the relations between Cree people and animals are established through stories (Feit 2004).

23 This belief contrasts with other Aboriginal conceptions, too. Writing about the Yukaghirs, Siberian elk hunters, Willerslev presents dramatic and graphic vignettes of hunters *becoming* animals through a process of mimesis in order to have hunting success (2007, 1).

24 My difficulty may have stemmed from my ineffective, even inappropriate, direct questioning. The ethnography of speaking is a useful method for uncovering ideas that people are reluctant to discuss openly.

25 *Tsesk'iye*, or crows and ravens, are common in Tahltan territory. According to the *Tahltan Children's Illustrated Dictionary*, *tsesk'iye* can refer to both crows and ravens (Carter, Carlick, and Carlick 1994, 128). In English, I routinely heard people refer to these black birds, regardless of size or call, as crows. In the Tahltan language, the Tahltan transformer and trickster is referred to as *Tsesk'iye Chō*. In English usage, this transformer is referred to as Big Crow or, more often, simply as Crow (*chō* is big). I do not hear Tahltan people using the name Raven to refer to Big Crow despite the fact that ravens are, in many ways, big crows. The rock bluff at the confluence of the Stikine and Tahltan Rivers is named, for example, *Tsesk'iye Cho Kime*, 'Big Crow's House.' People do not refer to this place as Raven's house.

These observations are complicated, but ultimately supported, by Teit's extensive record of Tahltan stories (Teit 1919; 1921a; 1921b). In the 1919 collection, Teit presents 'The Raven Cycle,' thirty-five stories of about Raven's activities in Tahltan territory. The first Raven story establishes the crow-raven confusion (Teit 1919, 198). In that story, called 'The Raven,' Teit's version says that Big-Raven (sic) is TsE'ketco (*Tsesk'iye Chō* in the contemporary orthography). A footnote follows: 'TsE'ketco or tcEski'tco, "big raven" (from tcEski'a, "raven"). When speaking English, the Tahltan generally call the Raven Transformer "Big-Crow"' (Teit 1919, 198). While Teit labelled tcEski'a (*tsesk'iye*) as raven, he is not incorrect. Further, Teit's observation of the Tahltan usage of 'crow' in reference to the transformer *Tsesk'iye Chō* is consistent with mine (and with Catharine McClellan's observations of Tagish usage [McClellan 1975, 173]). As a final note, Teit indicates that many of his Tahltan Raven stories originated with coastal Tlingits, for whom ravens are common and central to local narratives; the lengthy association of Tahltans at Telegraph Creek and Tlingits downriver on the Stikine is well-documented (e.g., Emmons 1911).

26 This is a political ecology in Wolf's sense of that phrase. For Wolf (1972), political ecology considers the relationship between politics, history, and multiple local and environmental contexts. Wolf writes: 'The local rules of ownership and inheritance are . . . not simply norms for the allocation of rights and obligations among a given population but mechanisms which mediate between the pressures emanating from the larger society and the exigencies of the local ecosystem' (Wolf 1972, 202).

27 Asch indicates that trapping became less viable in the Northwest Territories in the 1960s and 1970s because fur prices fell (Asch 1982, 364).

28 Feit observes a similar, second-era pattern among Quebec Crees. Feit calls their resistance to the construction of the Great Whale dam in the early 1970s 'anti-neo-liberal' (Feit 2010, 66) but notes that Cree control of their hunting and trapping territories had largely disappeared by this time (Feit 2004).

29 Other BC anthropologists have commented on the value of 'research by vehicle' (Palmer 1995; Dinwoodie 2002, 38) or on how difficult it can be to find oneself in constant demand as driver (Brody 1988).

30 In short, the term 'camping' is problematic. When outsiders hear 'going camping,' they may think of a weekend trip by car to any one of a number of possible locations. For the Iskut, camps are in effect homes; indeed, the Tahltan word *kime* means both camp and home. Hunting camps are symbolic of Iskut's permanent presence on the local landscape. Camps are places where families interact, pursue productive activities such as hunting and construction, and think about and encounter ancestors.

2. Iskut History and Hunting

1 The label Bear Lake (and its derivations, such as Bear Lakers, Bear Lake Nomads, Bear Lake Outpost) is extremely confusing (also Sheppard 1983b, 303–4). The confusion arises partly because there are Bear Lake Athapaskans in the Northwest Territories (Rushforth and Chisholm 1991) and another Bear Lake in the traditional territory of the Sekani Athapaskans along the Hart Highway north of Prince George, British Columbia. In short: Fort Connolly was on Bear Lake from 1826 to about 1900, and the Hudson's Bay Company referred to it also as Bear Lake Post. In the 1890s, the firm set up Fort Grahame on the Finlay River, 90 miles northeast of Fort Connolly (Patterson 1968, 84), to move the region's trapping centre and ease hostilities between rival Native groups (Sheppard 1983b, 311). As a result, the

company archives refer to Fort Grahame also as Bear Lake Outpost. Despite the potential confusion, Sheppard (1983b), following the work of Jenness (1937) and Morice (1894, 29; 1978 [1906]) and having reviewed the company's Fort Grahame journals, argues that the ancestors of most Iskut people lived at Fort Connolly on Bear Lake in the later nineteenth century.

2 The history of wage work at Iskut differs strikingly from that of some other BC Athapaskan groups. In Dakelh (Carrier) lands to the south of Iskut territory, Dakelh historians and anthropologists emphasize the total disruption of local economics and culture as a result of the fur trade and potlatch. In their work on acculturation among the Dakelh, Goldman (1941) and Steward (1960) describe how the potlatch came to central British Columbia from the Pacific coast in the early nineteenth century. The Dakelh adopted it because of the increased wealth available to some of their individuals and families through the fur trade (also Tobey 1981), and it became a primary means for disposing of wealth after an individual's death (also Fiske and Patrick 2000). As potlatching and fur trading increased, sustenance hunting became less important for acculturated Dakelh (also Murphy and Steward 1956). Hudson notes, however, a resurgence of bush economics and a reduction in potlatch economics once the fur trade declined. As a result, the shift to wage work was not complete (Hudson 1983). For the Iskut, because the fur trade of the nineteenth and early twentieth centuries focused on the Spatsizi Plateau, the potlatch has never become an institution, though it did find some hold in *Tlēgōhīn*, where Iskut people attended potlatches.

3 I do not know of a Tahltan-language place name for Caribou Hide.

4 My understanding and appreciation of the way places anchor people to tradition and history despite frequent movements comes from the work of Basso (1996), Palmer (2005), and Thornton (2008). In his masterful *Wisdom Sits in Places* (Basso 1996), Basso illustrates how Apache place names are fixtures on a cultural landscape that evoke memories, stories, and actions when those names are mentioned or heard even if one is removed from the named place. Basso writes about the process of 'speaking with names' (Basso 1996, 89), indicating: 'The place name (or names) that anchor a narrative can function reliably to evoke comparable images of ancestral events and corresponding appreciations of ancestral wisdom' (Basso 1996, 158). Palmer's *Maps of Experience* (Palmer 2005) details the uses of place names and stories by Secwepemc speakers in the context of colonialism and land claims. Palmer's work implicates the significance of anchoring history and tradition through talk, suggesting that 'various kinds of talk, situated in particular places on the landscape . . . allow knowledge to be carried

forward, reconstituted, reflected upon, enriched, and ultimately relocated, by and for new interlocutors, in new experiences, and sometimes new places' (Palmer 2005, 3). Thornton's work with Tlingit speakers emphasizes place names (Thornton 2008). But, his interest is not translation or documentation. Instead, Thornton is concerned with how place names inform and reflect local conceptions of the relationships between people and the lands on which they live (Thornton 2008, 70). All three of these scholars highlight the importance of linguistic analysis and the social use of talk. The significance is not simply that local landscapes are labelled with names, or even remain unnamed but historically significant; rather, the ways in which place names or stories of places and events are used create and maintain ties between history, place, tradition, and morality. For Iskut families, camps, old and new villages, trails, hunting areas, and, indeed, place names all anchor people to the land and, by extension, the past to the present. The stories presented in this book – stories of past hunts and guiding activities, and a speech that addresses contemporary politics – show the techniques by which Iskut people situate their present-day realities and concerns in historical events and memories.

5 Lanoue (1992) and Sheppard (1983b) are the key sources for understanding the history of the ethnic and family groups living north of Gitksan and Carrier groups, between the Rocky Mountain Trench (Finlay River) on the east and the Iskut River on the west. I do not intend to replicate their fine histories of this region, which are largely syntheses of Black (1824), Jenness (1937), Morice (1978 [1906]), and the journals of Hudson's Bay Company factors from places like Fort Grahame (eg., Anon. 1891–93). Further, Davis's book *The Sacred Headwaters* (2011b) provides a lyrical overview of Iskut history on the Spatsizi Plateau. Davis establishes the Iskut presence on the Spatsizi Plateau and uses that to discuss recent political events around Iskut; as such, his work has been helpful to me.

6 Sheppard, citing census records, notes that the Department of Indian Affairs began writing about Connolly Lake Sekanis in its records in 1893 (Sheppard 1983b, 313). The reification of a named ethnic group, one that identifies Native people at Bear Lake as something other than Tahltans or Sekanis proper, may date to this bureaucratic moment. Indeed, the Bear Lake label persists, as my opening vignette in this chapter suggests for 2000. Descendants of Sheppard's Iskut informants in the 1970s referred to themselves as the Bear Lake Indians.

7 Trapline registration may have affected the change in orientation from small, related nuclear families within hunting territories to group identification with the hunting territories themselves. Because the law required annual use

of a trapline or risking its loss, the Iskut orientation to territory may have shifted when hunters set up traplines in the 1920s. Indeed, the Iskut band owns a large trapline in the central part of the traditional territory.

8 For all species of plants, animals, fish, and birds, Tahltan names come from my field research and from Saxon (1997), Turner (1997), and Iskut First Nation (2005); equivalent species names in English and Latin are from Albright (1984) and Wooding (1997).

9 Since 2005, the region from which the Nass, Skeena, and Stikine rivers flow has become known as 'The Sacred Headwaters.' The importance of these rivers to Tahltans, downstream Native communities, and environmentalists stems from the large runs of salmon that use these rivers to travel from spawning grounds to the ocean and back (see Davis 2011a, b).

10 Vanstone (1974) notes the distinctions in Athapaskan food gathering for people who live in the Arctic Ocean or Pacific Ocean watersheds.

11 *Tl'abānot'ine* means 'people of the *Tl'abāne*' where *ot'ine* means 'people of.' These people are the *Tlepanoten* in Teit's research (Teit 1912–15a, b, 1956). Further details are provided in chapter 5.

12 *Tl'ogot'ine* means 'people of the [long] grass,' where *tl'oyh* is grass and *got'ine* means 'people of.' See chapter 5.

13 The moose populations may now be in significant decline. In September 2009, Iskut people blocked the access road into the Klappan Valley to non-Native hunters because they believed there were not enough moose to justify a hunt open to the public.

14 Morice (1978 [1906]), Jenness (1937), Walker (1976), Sheppard (1983a), and Lanoue (1992) detail this history.

15 Sheppard uses alternate and older labels, *T'lotona* for *Tl'ogot'ine* and *Tlepanoten* for *Tl'abānot'ine*. Sheppard's labels are probably Sekani in origin and they reflect the most common ways ethnographers have written about these groups (Teit 1912–15a, b; Jenness 1937, 13); see chapter 5.

16 MacLachlan says the mining venture was aborted (1956, 36). This is, however, one example of Iskut ancestors moving for potential wage work.

17 I was unable to record a Tahltan-language place name for Buckley Lake.

18 A road linking *Tatl'ah* with *Łuwechōn Menh* and Iskut was still a decade away.

19 The Commonage has several names in Iskut talk and in the literature. Some people call the place the Bear Lake Commonage. Others prefer the Iskut Commonage. Iskut families and Tahltans at *Tlēgōhīn* alike call it Yukon Side. This name contrasts directly with Kaska Side, the name for the Tahltan community on the north side of the river (also MacLachlan 1956). The people who lived there also acquired various appellations. In his *Tlēgōhīn* journal for 1956, MacLachlan refers to the Commonage residents

inconsistently, using both 'Bear Lakers' and 'Fort Grahame Nomads' (1956). Walker does the same in his extensive correspondence (various dates).

20 Not a pseudonym.

21 In the late 1970s, the park attracted the attention of Greenpeace, which protested against hunting there partly because of the contradiction between hunting and preservation of a wilderness area. *The Fifth Estate* documented the conflict in a documentary of 17 November 1981 (Canadian Broadcasting Corporation 1981).

22 Tahltan people have not been passive observers of mining and other developments in their territory. For example, the establishment in 1985 of the Tahltan Nation Development Corporation (TNDC) complicates the story of recent Tahltan involvement in resource development. TNDC acquires contracts to build roads, provide ancillary services like food services to mines, and, more generally, oversee economic development in the area. In a fishery strategy aimed at increasing the participation of Tahltans in a commercial fishery, TNDC's goals for local-level development include employment and the economic viability of Tahltan businesses (Cassidy and Dale 1988, 56–57). Writing in the late 1980s, at the time of negotiations between the Tahltan leadership and Gulf Canada over the development of coal mines, Cassidy and Dale wonder if the Tahltan will adopt a partnership or an adversarial arrangement with Gulf (153–54). More recently, the Tahltan Central Council negotiated a revenue-sharing agreement with Teck and NovaGold related to a mine at Galore Creek. While the mine development has been slowed by a faltering economy, the agreement indicates to some that Tahltans are willing participants in mining activities. My observations suggest that the type of relationship that is established between Tahltans and industrial developers is dependent as much on how development is regarded by the Tahltan leaders of the day as it is on the perceived impacts of the project (e.g., Paulson 2006). And events like the arrests of protesters from Iskut in 2005 and 2006 blocking Royal Dutch Shell from the *Tl'abāne* suggest strongly that local opposition to mining is not seen favourably by British Columbia courts or the provincial government.

3. Food Animals and Traditional Knowledge

1 An earlier version of this chapter appeared as an article in the journal *Anthropological Linguistics* (McIlwraith 2008).

2 *Kime* translates to both camp and home. This camp is located at *Didini Tū'e*.

3 Speaking about Siberian pastoralists, Anderson says that the mutual interrelation between people and places constructs a sentient ecology.

It is an important idea because, says Anderson, it departs from classical ecological anthropological theory by assigning agency to the natural world (Anderson 2002, 116–17).

4 I have received support for the phrase 'serious chatter' from some Athapaskanists, while others have questioned its significance to Iskut people and wondered if there was a better, locally meaningful phrase to use. 'Serious chatter' is my attempt to characterize what I hear happening in these stories. To date, I have not identified a suitable Tahltan word or phrase for this kind of conversation-as-story about hunting.

5 I do not have any recordings of similar stories in the Tahltan language.

6 Following Palmer (2005), line breaks in the transcript are prompted by pauses in speech. Each line represents, in effect, a single utterance (also Brown and Yule 1983).

7 While Iskut people call them 'groundhogs' in English, the animals are identified as marmots by biologists (*Marmota monax petrensis* or *Marmota caligata*).

8 Frank is Arthur's younger brother.

9 The withers is the hump on the back of the moose to which muscles attach. Iskut hunters pronounce this feature as 'the weathers' or call it the 'weather bone.' The Tahltan word is *eghane*. The two speakers say 'weather bone' at lines 26 and 27 at the same time.

10 Scotty is Arthur's cousin.

11 I have written this word in the conventions of the Tahltan practical orthography in hopes of replicating the sound that Arthur uses when mimicking the firing of a rifle. The letter i is pronounced as in the English word *bit* (IPA symbol [I]), and *ū* like the vowel sound in the English word *boot*.

12 The lake is about ten miles north of Iskut Village. It is spelled 'Morchuea' on government-issued topographic maps.

13 While this chapter focuses on stories about pursuing moose, the structure and content of these stories often includes other animals like caribou or even grouse.

14 Henry S. Sharp offers an answer in his reflections on fieldwork with Chipewyan hunters. Concerning a loon that refused to succumb to a Chipewyan hunter's repeated attempts to shoot it, he notes: 'The loon was not merely refusing to sacrifice itself to the hunters, it was exhibiting its power ... The refusal of an animal to sacrifice itself produces no sense of fear or anxiety on the part of the Chipewyan. In this environment they would not have long survived as people if individuals reacted strongly every time they encountered an animal that was not willing to die for them. They are, however, chagrined when it happens' (2001, 91). In other

words, simply behaving properly does not guarantee hunting success. The choice to die remains with the animal, which sometimes refuses to fall for its own opaque reasons.

15 A pseudonym.

16 *Ensuge* is literally 'your fart.' *En* is a second-person pronoun, and *suge* is 'fart.' *Dintsełis* 'you will eat.'

17 Martha James says that the punishment of hunters by animals does not occur today. For Martha, such talk is a vestige of the past. Martha admits, however, that interdictions like 'you're gonna starve' may be used to scare children who are wasteful with their food. Peg James also shrugs off talk of traditions like thanking animals for their sacrifice as simply a behaviour from the past. 'People used to thank everything,' she says. These traditions have changed, to be sure, particularly in light of Christian teachings about prayer, God as a creator, and animals that are put on earth to serve people rather than the other way around. Some elders admitted to me, however, that they believe *Tsesk'iye Chō*, 'Big Crow,' who created the world and the animals is the Christian God. Two systems of belief about animals appear to blend into one for some people.

4. Work Animals and Guiding Work

1 Sharp details the differences between dogs and wolves in Chipewyan experience and thought (2001, 83–90; 1976).

2 These sentences are from a letter by Iskut leaders to J.V. Boys, Indian Commissioner for British Columbia; Robin Kendall, regional supervisor for fisheries and wildlife in British Columbia and Yukon; and Arthur Laing, federal minister of Northern Affairs (later Indian Affairs and now Aboriginal Affairs and Northern Development Canada). The leaders wrote it in response to poor living conditions at Iskut shortly after several families moved there from Telegraph Creek (*Tlēgōhīn*) (Walker, various dates, MS-2784, box 18, file 3). The names attributed to the epigraph are not pseudonyms.

3 Derr speculates that the Tahltan Bear Dog became extinct in the 1970s or 1980s. Derr writes that the animal was 'rendered obsolete by high-powered repeating rifles that made killing bears a relatively easy, long distance affair' (Derr 1997, 54). To extend Derr's analysis, I would add that other technological advances in hunting, like the use of all-terrain vehicles and snowmobiles, lessened the need for dogs as work animals.

4 Teit recorded Tahltan versions of this story (1909, 318; 1921a, 248–50). Sheppard discusses this tale at Iskut as well as its distribution throughout northern Canada (1983a). Amoss describes the Dog Husband story

and its myth-time context on the northwest coast. The story indicates, says Amoss, that dogs are inappropriate marriage partners because they are associated closely with families; these marriages would usually be considered incestuous. In contrast, marriages between people and other animals (animal-persons) are permissible although dangerous (Amoss 1984, 299–304). Other animals represent outsiders, or, exogamous marriage partners.

5 Basso discusses Apache commemorative place names in *Wisdom Sits in Places*: 'Commemorative in character and linked to traditional stories, [commemorative place names] allude to historical events that illuminate the causes and consequences of wrongful social conduct ... they invest the Apache landscape with a sobering moral dimension, dark but instructive, that place markers can exploit to deeply telling effect' (Basso 1996, 23–24).

6. *Deneka'ladiyah* is a place name. See Appendix for more information.

7 Sharp says that the Chipewyan 'call the coyote by a diminutive of the word for wolf and pay little attention to it' (2001, 75).

8 Amoss identifies the basis for such ambiguity in groups on the northwest coast: 'Northwest peoples recognized that the dog was closely related to wild *Canidae*, wolves, foxes, and coyotes. At the same time, dogs lived in the human household, shared human food, and as companions in the hunt took mankind's part against the beasts of the wild. Depending on whether the principles of classification were functional or morphological the dog could fit into the human or animal category (Amoss 1984, 292). She elaborates by saying that dogs are the most aberrant member of the category of animal because they live with people; in other words, on the northwest coast, there is no category of domestication (293).

9 Alec Jack was a Gitksan man who married into an Iskut family. He spent much of his life on the Spatsizi Plateau and in Iskut (Davis 2001, 27–31).

10 Scott and Webber describe the experiences of Cree outfitters in northern Quebec and note the complexity of the situation there. There are Crees who support outfitting and participate extensively. They argue that participation is a means of controlling hunting and economic development. Cree hunters who want hunting for sport banned see it as incompatible with Cree traditions on ethical and economic grounds; sport hunting is not a reasonable way to make a living given the relationships Crees have with animals (Scott and Webber 2001, 167–68).

11 Scott and Webber write that Cree sustenance hunters become upset by sports hunting even if the animals are abundant and rules governing the

hunts are in place. Despite sufficient game, some Cree hunters consider sport hunting as an invasion into their territory (Scott and Webber 2001, 163).

12 Feit and Asch write about a similar process whereby hunters quickly embraced wage-based trapping and hunting in other parts of northern Canada. Asch writes about the Dene of the Northwest Territories (Asch 1982, 362) and Feit, the Cree of Quebec (Feit 2010, 55). Tanner suggests that mercantilism and sustenance hunting are not in conflict among the Quebec Crees that he studied (Tanner 1979, 9–10).

13 Feit notes that the narratives from the guiding era draw on episodes of conflict and co-existence between Natives and non-Native business owners (2010, 55). In his stories about guiding and Walker, Robert balances those two extremes.

5. Chief Louie's Speech at Spatsizi Plateau Wilderness Park

1 BC Parks runs the camp today. A caretaker lives in one cabin during summer and maintains the cabins, a large kitchen and dining hall, pit toilets, a warehouse, and a dock.

2 Regna Darnell has written extensively about indigenous cultures and communities in flux or transition in Canada. With reference to the experiences of Algonquian-speaking groups in southern Ontario, Darnell posits an 'accordion model' in which indigenous people move in and out of home communities as the needs of everyday life, including the search for food and other resources and trade, demand. She writes: 'the basic model of Algonquian social organization is not one of random movement on land but of an accordion, a process of subsistence-motivated expansion and contraction of social groups in relation to resource exploitation' (Darnell 1998, 91). Moving successfully, as Darnell puts it, is a hallmark of both Algonquian and Athapaskan communities (91).

Beyond a characterization of the traditional patterns of territorial movements of foragers, the accordion model reflects the impositions and requirements of colonialism, including the requirement that Native people live on reserves. As indigenous communities became fixed on reserves, people moved in and out of these places often for wage work: 'What anthropologists have [previously] characterized as band, tribe, community, and nation reflect shifting moments in . . . pragmatic decisions. The number of people who live in a given home place follows a cycle of contraction and expansion through the individual life cycle and in relation to ongoing obligations within the public life of the home community. The accordion retains its flexibility and adaptability' (Darnell 1998, 104; also 2009, 6). The accordion model applies to the community at Iskut Village, where a mobile population comes and goes as necessary all the while maintaining some form of relationship with the village location and surrounding territory that might be defined as home.

3 For Anthony D. Smith, 'an "ethnic group" is a type of community with a specific sense of solidarity and honor, and a set of shared symbols and values' (1981, 65).

4 Indeed, in 2009 the Liberal BC government sought to reorganize all Native groups in the province into thirty 'tribes' to streamline treaty negotiations.

5 These statements refer presumably to Tommy Walker. They may also relate to others – including non-Iskut Tahltans – who have questioned Iskut's claim to the Spatsizi.

6 Jenness notes that speakers of Sekani refer to the *Tl'ogot'ine* as *T'lotona*. Jenness also says that speakers of Tahltan use the ethnonym *T'lukotene* for the *Tl'ogot'ine* (Jenness 1937, 13; also Sheppard 1983b, 335; also Teit 1912–15a, b). These names are cognates, and the pronunciations are not that different. Still, the variations in spelling add confusion to understanding what groups have been present in the area.

7 Anthony D. Smith notes that a land base or homeland is a defining characteristic of an ethnic *nation* (1981, 69) but that land is not necessary for an assertion of ethnic *community* (66). Nationhood includes, by definition, a sense of territoriality (also 164). In these terms, Iskut collectively might be a community but not a nation.

8 A representative from the Tahltan Central Council from Dease Lake came along and stayed only briefly. Perhaps he wanted to reinforce political connections with the visitors and to acknowledge that claims on the Spatsizi region extend beyond those of the Iskut First Nation.

9 This is Chief Louie's reaction to BC settlers' claims of a *terra nullius*. In *Delgamuukw v. The Queen* (1997), prior occupancy was cited as a basis for Aboriginal rights and land title in the province (also Culhane 1998).

6. Everyday Talk about Hunting

1 The recent history of protests against Shell and other resource development companies is detailed in Davis (2011b).

2 Blaser et al. (2010, 3–4) complain that the discussions and debates about globalization rarely involve indigenous peoples and their experiences.

3 A Tahltan politician once asked me, rhetorically, how many mining jobs were actually needed to serve Tahltan people. In the politician's view,

the pitch of mining jobs in exchange for the support of new mines rang hollow because there is only a limited number of Tahltans actually looking for such work.

4 The pragmatic interest in embracing change from development or opposing it is a significant theme in Feit's writings about the Quebec Cree. See, for example, Feit (2010, 51; 2004, 107).

References

Adlam, Robert G. 1985. 'The Structural Basis of Tahltan Indian Society.' PhD diss., University of Toronto.
– 1995. 'The Dog Husband and "Dirty" Woman: The Cultural Context of a Traditional Tahltan Narrative.' *Igitur* 6–7, no. 2/1:39–57.
Akrigg, G.P.V., and Helen B. Akrigg. 1997. *British Columbia Place Names.* Vancouver: UBC Press.
Albright, Sylvia. 1984. *Tahltan Ethnoarchaeology.* Publication 15. Burnaby, BC: Department of Archaeology, Simon Fraser University.
Alderete, John. 2005. 'On Tone and Length in Tahltan.' In *Athabaskan Prosody,* ed. Sharon Hargus and Keren Rice. Amsterdam: John Benjamins.
Alderete, John, and Thomas McIlwraith. 2008. 'An Annotated Bibliography of Tahltan Language Materials.' *Northwest Journal of Linguistics* 2, no. 1:1–26.
Amoss, Pamela. 1984. 'A Little More than Kin, and Less than Kind: The Ambiguous Northwest Coast Dog.' In *The Tsimshian and Their Neighbors of the North Pacific Coast,* ed. Jay Miller and Carol M. Eastman. Seattle: University of Washington Press.
Anon. 5 September 2006. 'The Road Less Travelled: Living on the Alaska Highway.' *Where All the World's Wild Rebels Are.* http://wickerchair.blogspot.com/2006/09/road-less-travelled-living-on-alaska.html.
– 30 December 2006. 'An Apology to Dease Lake.' http://wickerchair.blogspot.com/2006/12/apology-to-dease-lake.html
Anon. 1891–93. Journal, Fort Grahame Post. Winnipeg: Hudson's Bay Company Archives, B/249/a/1.
Anderson, David G. 2002. *Identity and Ecology in Arctic Siberia: The Number One Reindeer Brigade.* New York: Oxford University Press.
Asch, Michael. 1982. 'Dene Self-Determination and the Study of Hunter-Gatherers in the Modern World.' In *Politics and History in Band Societies,*

ed. Eleanor Leacock and Richard B. Lee. New York: Cambridge University Press.

Barker, John. 2007. *Ancestral Lines: The Maisin of Papua New Guinea and the Fate of the Rainforest.* Toronto: University of Toronto Press.

Basso, Keith H. 1996. *Wisdom Sits in Places: Landscape and Language among the Western Apache.* Albuquerque: University of New Mexico Press.

Bauman, Richard. 1986. *Story, Performance, Event: Contextual Studies of Oral Narrative.* New York: Cambridge University Press.

Bauman, Richard, and Joel Sherzer. 1974. *Explorations in the Ethnography of Speaking.* New York: Cambridge University Press.

Berkes, Fikret. 1999. *Sacred Ecology: Traditional Ecological Knowledge and Resource Management.* Philadelphia: Taylor and Francis.

Berkhofer, Robert F. 1978. *The White Man's Indian.* Toronto: Random House.

Berlin, Brent. 1966. 'Folk Taxonomies and Biological Classification.' *Science* 154, no. 3746:273–75.

Black, Samuel. 1824. 'A Voyage of Discovery from the Rocky Mountain Portage on the Peace River to the Sources of the Finlays Branch and North-westward, Summer 1824.' BCARS Add Mss 619, typescript. BC Archives and Records Service, Victoria.

Blaser, Mario, Ravi de Costa, Deborah McGregor, and William D. Coleman. 2010. 'Reconfiguring the Web of Life: Indigenous Peoples, Relationality, and Globalization.' In *Indigenous Peoples and Autonomy: Insights for a Global Age,* ed. Mario Blaser, Ravi de Costa, Deborah McGregor, and William D. Coleman. Vancouver: UBC Press.

Bob, Tanya. 1999. 'Laryngeal Phenomena in Tahltan.' MA thesis, University of British Columbia.

Braroe, Neils W. 1975. *Indian and White: Self-Image and Interaction in a Canadian Plains Community.* Stanford, CA: Stanford University Press.

Briggs, Charles L. 1993. 'Generic versus Metapragmatic Dimensions of Warao Narratives: Who Regiments Performance?' In *Reflexive Language: Reported Speech and Metapragmatics,* ed. John A. Lucy. Cambridge: Cambridge University Press.

Brightman, Robert A. 1993. *Grateful Prey: Rock Cree Human-Animal Relationships.* Berkeley and Los Angeles: University of California Press.

British Columbia v. Haida Nation et al. 2004. Reasons for Judgment. Decision of the Supreme Court of Canada ([2004] 3 S.C.R. 511, 2004 SCC 73).

Brody, Hugh. 1988. *Maps and Dreams: Indians and the British Columbia Frontier.* Vancouver: Douglas and McIntyre.

– 2000. *The Other Side of Eden: Hunters, Farmers, and the Shaping of the World.* New York: North Point Press.

Brown, Gillian, and George Yule. 1983. *Discourse Analysis*. New York: Cambridge University Press.

Canada. Department of Indian Affairs. 1930. *Stikine Area Census: 1930*. Union of BC Indian Chiefs, Vancouver.

Canadian Broadcasting Corporation. 1981. 'The Fifth Estate: Greenpeace Takes on Hunters in Spatsizi Park.' Broadcast date: 17 November 1981. (http://archives.cbc.ca/environment/environmental_protection/topics/867-5037/)

Careless, Ric. 1997. *To Save the Wild Earth: Field Notes from the Environmental Frontier*. Vancouver: Raincoast Books.

Carlson, Keith T. 1997. *You Are Asked to Witness: The Sto:lo in Canada's Pacific Coast History*. Chilliwack, BC: Sto:lo Heritage Trust.

Carmichael, Amy. 2005. 'Nine Elders of Tahltan First Nation Arrested Trying to Block Mining Company.' Canadian Press, 16 September 2005.

Carpentier, Father. 1938–46. Codex Historicus of Telegraph Creek Mission and the Dependent Missions of Cariboo Hide, Tskut Lake, Dease Lake, Sheslay. Deschatelets Archives, Ottawa.

Carter, Colin. 1991. *Basic Tahltan Conversation Lessons (Text and Tape)*. *Tatl'ah*: Tahltan Tribal Council; prepared in collaboration with Patrick Carlick (*Tlēgōhīn*), Angela Dennis and Regina Louie (Iskut), Susie Tashoots and Myra Blackburn (*Tatl'ah*), Freddie Quock, and Edith Carlick.

Carter, Colin, Patrick Carlick, and Edith Carlick. 1994. *The Tahltan Children's Illustrated Dictionary*. Dease Lake: Tahltan Tribal Council; prepared in collaboration with Patrick Carlick (*Tlēgōhīn*), Angela Dennis and Regina Louie (Iskut), Susie Tashoots and Myra Blackburn (*Tatl'ah*), Freddie Quock, and Edith Carlick.

Cassidy, Frank, and Norman Dale. 1988. *After Native Claims: The Implications of Comprehensive Claims Settlements for Natural Resources in British Columbia*. Lantzville, BC: Oolichan Books and the Institute for Research on Public Policy.

Coates, Ken S. 1991. *Best Left as Indians: Native-White Relations in the Yukon Territory, 1840–1973*. Montreal: McGill-Queen's University Press.

Colpitts, George W. 2002. *Game in the Garden: A Human History of Wildlife in Western Canada to 1940*. Vancouver: UBC Press.

Conklin, Harold C. 1954. 'The Relation of Hanunoo Culture to the Plant World.' PhD diss., Yale University.

Coupland, Justine. 2003. 'Small Talk: Social Functions.' *Research on Language and Social Interaction* 36, no. 1:1–6.

Crapanzano, Vincent. 1996. '"Self-Centering Narratives.' In *Natural Histories of Discourse*, ed. Michael Silverstein and Greg Urban. Chicago: University of Chicago Press.

Cruikshank, Julie. 1990. *Life Lived Like a Story: Life Stories of Three Yukon Elders.* Lincoln: University of Nebraska Press.

– 1998a. *The Social Life of Stories: Narrative and Knowledge in the Yukon Territory.* Lincoln: University of Nebraska Press.

– 1998b. 'Yukon Arcadia.' In *The Social Life of Stories: Narrative and Knowledge in the Yukon Territory.* Lincoln: University of Nebraska Press.

– 2005. *Do Glaciers Listen? Local Knowledge, Colonial Encounters, and Social Imagination.* Vancouver: UBC Press.

Culhane, Dara. 1998. *The Pleasure of the Crown: Anthropology, Law, and First Nations.* Vancouver: Talonbooks.

Darnell, Regna. 1998. 'Rethinking Band and Tribe, Community and Nation: An Accordion Model of Nomadic Native North American Social Organization.' In *Papers of the 29th Algonquian Conference.*

– 2009. Cross-Cultural Constructions of Work, Leisure and Community Responsibility: Some First Nations Reflections. *Journal of Occupational Science* 16, no. 1:4–9.

Davis, Wade. 2001. *Light at the Edge of the World.* Toronto: Douglas and McIntyre.

– 2011a. Violating the Sacred. *Alternatives Journal* 37, no. 1:24–28.

– 2011b. *The Sacred Headwaters: The Fight to Save the Stikine, Skeena, and Nass.* Vancouver: D&M Publishers.

Dawson, George M. 1888. *Report on an Exploration in the Yukon District, N.W.T. and Adjacent Northern Portion of British Columbia, 1887.* Montreal: Dawson Brothers.

Delgamuukw v. The Queen. 1991. Reasons for Judgment. Decision of the Supreme Court of British Columbia ([1991] Index number: 0400.91, No.: 0843).

Delgamuukw v. The Queen. 1997. Reasons for Judgment. Decision of the Supreme Court of Canada ([1997] 3 S.C.R. 1010, 1997, CanLII 302 [S.C.C.]).

Derr, Mark. 1997. *Dog's Best Friend: Annals of the Dog-Human Relationship.* Chicago: University of Chicago Press.

Dinwoodie, David. 2002. *Reserve Memories: The Power of the Past in a Chilcotin Community.* Lincoln: University of Nebraska Press.

Duff, Wilson. 1965. *The Indian History of British Columbia: The Impact of the White Man.* Memoir no. 5. Victoria: Royal British Columbia Museum.

Duranti, Alessandro. 1997. *Linguistic Anthropology.* New York: Cambridge University Press.

Ellen, Roy F. 1986. 'Ethnobiology, Cognition, and the Structure of Prehension: Some General Theoretical Notes.' *Journal of Ethnobiology* 6, no. 1:83–98.

Emmons, G. T. 1911. *The Tahltan Indians.* Philadelphia: University of Pennsylvania Press.

Feit, Harvey A. 2004. 'James Bay Crees' Life Projects and Politics: Histories of Place, Animal Partners and Enduring Relationships.' In *In the Way of Development: Indigenous Peoples, Life Projects and Globalization,* ed. Mario Blaser, Harvey A. Feit, and Glenn McRae. London: Zed Books/IDRC.

– 2010. 'Neoliberal Governance and James Bay Cree Co-Governance: Negotiated Agreements, Oppositional Struggles, and Co-Governance.' In *Indigenous Peoples and Autonomy: Insights for a Global Age,* ed. Mario Blaser, Ravi de Costa, Deborah McGregor, and William D. Coleman. Vancouver: UBC Press.

Finnegan, Ruth. 1992. *Oral Traditions and the Verbal Arts: A Guide to Research Practices.* New York: Routledge.

Fisher, Robin. 1977. *Contact and Conflict: Indian-European Relations in British Columbia, 1774–1890.* Vancouver: UBC Press.

Fiske, Jo-Anne, and Betty Patrick. 2000. *Cis Dideen Kat: When the Plume Rises.* Vancouver: UBC Press.

Foster, Hamar. 1998. 'Honouring the Queen: A Legal and Historical Perspective on the Nisga'a Treaty.' *BC Studies.* 120, no. 4:11–35.

Frake, Charles O. 1980 [1962]. 'Cultural Ecology and Ethnography.' In *Language and Cultural Description.* Stanford, CA: Stanford University Press.

Francis, Daniel. 1992. *The Imaginary Indian: The Image of the Indian in Canadian Culture.* Vancouver: Arsenal Pulp Press.

Frankfurt, Harry. 1986. 'On Bullshit.' *Raritan* 6:81–100.

Friesen, David E. 1985. 'Aboriginal Settlement Patterns in the Upper Stikine River Drainage, Northwestern British Columbia.' MA thesis, University of Calgary.

Furniss, Elizabeth. 1999. *The Burden of History: Colonialism and the Frontier Myth in a Rural Canadian Community.* Vancouver: UBC Press.

Geertz, Clifford. 1973. 'Thick Description: Toward an Interpretive Theory of Culture.' In *The Interpretation of Cultures.* New York: Basic Books.

– 1983. *Local Knowledge: Further Essays in Interpretive Anthropology.* New York: Basic Books.

Goffman, Erving. 1963. *Stigma: Notes on the Management of Spoiled Identity.* Englewood Cliffs, NJ: Prentice-Hall.

– 1981. *Forms of Talk.* Philadelphia: University of Pennsylvania Press.

– 1986. *Frame Analysis: An Essay on the Organization of Experience.* Boston: Northeastern University Press.

Goldman, Irving. 1941. 'The Alkatcho Carrier: Historical Background of Crest Prerogatives.' *American Anthropologist* 43, no. 3:396–418.

Goulet, Jean-Guy A. 1998. *Ways of Knowing: Experience, Knowledge, and Power among the Dene Tha.* Lincoln: University of Nebraska Press.

Gumperz, John J. 1972. 'The Speech Community.' In *Language and Social Context,* ed. Pier P. Giglioli. New York: Penguin.

Hallowell, A.I. 1960. 'Ojibwa Ontology, Behavior, and World View.' In *Culture in History: Essays in Honor of Paul Radin,* ed. Stanley Diamond. New York: Columbia University Press.

Hardwick, Margaret. 1984. 'Tahltan Consonant Harmony.' In *Papers of the XIX International Conference on Salishan and Neighboring Languages.* Victoria: University of Victoria Press.

Hawkes, David T. 1966. 'An Analysis of Demographic Data Dealing with Employment and Residence Patterns in the Two Indian Communities of *Tlēgōhīn* and Iskut, British Columbia.' BA essay, University of British Columbia. BC Archives, MS-0858.

Helm, June. 1965. '"Bilaterality" in the Socio-Territorial Organization of the Arctic Drainage Dene.' *Ethnology* 4:361–85.

Henderson, Bob. 2006. *In the Land of the Red Goat.* Smithers, BC: Creekstone Press.

Honigmann, John J. 1946. Ethnography and Acculturation of the Fort Nelson Slave. New Haven, CT: Yale University Press.

– 1949. *Culture and Ethos of Kaska Society.* New Haven, CT: Yale University Press.

Hubert, Henri, and Marcel Mauss. 1964 [1898]. *Sacrifice: Its Nature and Function.* Chicago: University of Chicago Press.

Hudson, Douglas R. 1983. 'Traplines and Timber: Social and Economic Change among the Carrier Indians of Northern British Columbia.' PhD diss., University of Alberta.

Hunn, Eugene S. 1990. *Nch'i-Wana: Mid-Columbia Indians and Their Land.* Seattle: University of Washington Press.

Hymes, Dell H. 1962. 'The Ethnography of Speaking.' In *Anthropology and Human Behavior.* Washington, DC: Anthropological Society of Washington.

– 1975. 'Breakthrough into Performance.' In *Folklore: Performance and Communication,* ed. Dan Ben-Amos and Kenneth S. Goldstein The Hague: Mouton.

– 1981. *'In vain I tried to tell you': Essays in Native American Ethnopoetics.* Philadelphia: University of Pennsylvania Press.

Ingold, Tim. 2000. 'Culture, Nature, Environment: Steps to the Ecology of Life.' In *The Perception of the Environment: Essays on Livelihood, Dwelling and Skill.* New York: Routledge.

Iskut First Nation. 2005. 'Traditional Medicines and Remedies of the Iskut People.' Iskut: Typescript held by the Iskut Health Centre.

Jarvenpa, Robert. 1998. *Northern Passage: Ethnography and Apprenticeship among the Subarctic Dene.* Prospect Heights, IL: Waveland Press.

Jenness, Diamond. 1937. *The Sekani Indians of British Columbia.* Ottawa: Department of Mines and Resources.

Kaska Tribal Council. 1997. *Guzâgi K'úgé' Our Language Book: Nouns. Kaska, Mountain Slavey and Sekani.* Whitehorse: Kaska Tribal Council.

Keating, Elizabeth. 2001. 'The Ethnography of Communication.' In *Handbook of Ethnography,* ed. Paul Atkinson, Amanda Coffey, Sara Delamont, John Lofland, Lyn Lofland. London: Sage Publications.

Kerr, F.A. 1929. 'Preliminary Report on Iskut River Area, B.C. (Part A).' Ottawa: Geological Survey of Canada.

Labov, William. 1972. 'The Social Motivation of a Sound Change.' In *Sociolinguistic Patterns.* Philadelphia: University of Pennsylvania Press.

Lanoue, Guy. 1990. 'Breakdown and Ethnographic Consciousness: The Sekani Case.' *European Review of Native Studies* 4, no. 2:45–52.

– 1992. *Brothers: The Politics of Violence among the Sekani of Northern British Columbia.* New York: Berg.

Leer, Jeff. 1985. 'A Recommendation for the Tahltan Practical Orthography.' Alaska Native Language Center, University of Alaska. Typescript.

Levi-Strauss, Claude. 1963. *Structural Anthropology.* New York: Basic Books.

– 1966 [1962]. *The Savage Mind.* Chicago: University of Chicago Press.

Loo, Tina. 2001a. 'Making a Modern Wilderness: Conserving Wildlife in Twentieth-Century Canada.' *Canadian Historical Review* 82, no. 1:91–121.

– 2001b. 'Of Moose and Men: Hunting for Masculinities in British Columbia, 1880–1939.' *Western Historical Quarterly* 32, no. 3:269–319.

– 2006. *States of Nature: Conserving Canada's Wildlife in the Twentieth Century.* Vancouver: UBC Press.

Lutz, John S. 2008. *Makuk: A New History of Aboriginal-White Relations.* Vancouver: UBC Press.

MacLachlan, Bruce B. 1956. Journal and Fieldnotes from *Tlēgōhīn,* Summer 1956. Received from Janice Sheppard in 2005.

– 1981. 'Tahltan.' In *Handbook of North American Indians, Vol. 6: Subarctic,* ed. June Helm. Washington, DC: Smithsonian Institution Press.

Magnusson, Warren, and Karena Shaw. 2003. *A Political Space: Reading the Global through Clayoquot Sound.* Minneapolis: University of Minnesota Press.

Manelis Klein, Harriet E. 1999. 'Narrative.' *Journal of Linguistic Anthropology* 9, no. 1–2:167–69.

Martin, Calvin. 1978. *Keepers of the Game: Indian-Animal Relationships and the Fur Trade.* Berkeley and Los Angeles: University of California Press.

McClellan, Catharine. 1975. *My Old People Say: An Ethnographic Survey of Southern Yukon Territory.* Ottawa: National Museum of Man.

McIlwraith, Thomas. 2007. 'But We Are Still Native People: Speaking of Hunting and History in a Northern Athapaskan Village.' PhD diss., University of New Mexico.

– 2008. '"The Bloody Moose Got Up and Took Off": Talking Carefully about Food Animals in a Northern Athabaskan Village.' *Anthropological Linguistics* 50, no. 2:125–47.

McKee, Christopher. 2000. *Treaty Talks in British Columbia: Negotiating a Mutually Beneficial Future*. Vancouver: UBC Press.

Mears, Daniel P. 2002. 'The Ubiquity, Functions, and Contexts of Bullshitting.' *Journal of Mundane Behavior* 3, no. 2:233–56.

Menzies, Charles R. 1994. 'Stories from Home: First Nations, Land Claims, and Euro-Canadians.' *American Ethnologist* 21, no. 4:776–91.

Menzies, Charles R., and Caroline Butler. 2006. 'Understanding Local Ecological Knowledge.' In *Local Level Ecological Knowledge and Natural Resource Management*, ed. Charles R. Menzies. Lincoln: University of Nebraska Press.

Miller, Bruce G., ed. 1992. *Anthropology and History in the Courts (Special Issue). BC Studies* 95 (autumn).

Moore, Patrick. 2002. 'Point of View in Kaska Historical Narratives.' PhD diss., University of Indiana.

– 2007. 'Poking Fun: Humour and Power in Kaska Contact Narratives.' In *Myth and Memory: Stories of Indigenous–European Contact*, ed. John S. Lutz. Vancouver: UBC Press.

Moore, Robert E. 1993. 'Performance Form and the Voices of Characters in Five Versions of the Wasco Coyote Cycle.' In *Reflexive Language: Reported Speech and Metapragmatics*, ed. John A. Lucy. Cambridge: Cambridge University Press.

Moran, Emilio F. 2000. *Human Adaptability: An Introduction to Ecological Anthropology*. Boulder, CO: Westview Press.

Morgan, Ellen. 2009. 'Contesting Development: Neoliberalism, Indigenous Rights and Environmental Governance in the Sacred Headwaters.' MA thesis, University of Oxford.

Morice, A.G. 1894. 'Notes Archaeological, Industrial, and Sociological on the Western Denes.' *Transactions of the Canadian Institute, 1892–1893* Part I (1):1–222.

– 1978 [1906]. *The History of the Northern Interior of British Columbia*. Smithers, BC: Interior Stationery.

Mouchet, Father J.-M. 2002. *Men and Women of the Tundra*. Whitehorse, YT: Arctic Raven Publishing.

Murphy, Robert, and Julian Steward. 1956. 'Tappers and Trappers: Parallel Processes in Acculturation.' *Economic Development and Cultural Change* 4, no. 1:335–55.

Nadasdy, Paul. 1999. 'The Politics of TEK: Power and the "Integration" of Knowledge.' *Arctic Anthropology* 36, no. 1–2:1–18.

– 2003. *Hunters and Bureaucrats: Power, Knowledge, and Aboriginal-State Relations in the Southwest Yukon*. Vancouver: UBC Press.

– 2005. 'Transcending the Debate over the Ecologically Noble Indian: Indigenous People and Environmentalism.' *Ethnohistory* 52, no. 2:291–331.

– 2007. 'The Gift in the Animal: The Ontology of Hunting and Human-Animal Sociality.' *American Ethnologist* 34, no. 1:25–43.

Nater, Hank F. 1989. 'Some Comments on the Phonology of Tahltan.' *International Journal of American Linguistics* 55, no. 1:25–42.

Nazarea, Virginia D., ed. 1999. *Ethnoecology: Situated Knowledge/Located Lives.* Tucson: University of Arizona Press.

Neering, Rosemary. 1989. *Continental Dash: The Russian-American Telegraph.* Ganges, BC: Horsdal and Schubart.

Palmer, Andie. 2005. *Maps of Experience: The Anchoring of Land to Story in Secwepemc Discourse.* Toronto: University of Toronto Press.

Patterson, R.M. 1968. *Finlay's River.* Toronto: MacMillan.

Paulson, Monte. 2006. 'A Gentle Revolution.' *Walrus* 2, no. 10:64–75.

Peirce, Charles. 1992. 'What Is a Sign?' In *The Essential Peirce: Selected Philosophical Writings Vol. 2 (1893–1913),* ed. Nathan Houser and Christian Kloesel. Bloomington: Indiana University Press.

Polster, D.F., and L.J. Pituley. 1994. 'Mount Klappan Coal Project: 10 Years of Reclamation Experience in Northwestern BC.' In *Proceedings of the 18th Annual British Columbia Mine Reclamation Symposium.* Victoria: Ministry of Energy, Mines and Petroleum Resources, Technical and Research Committee on Reclamation (British Columbia), Mining Association of British Columbia, and Ministry of Environment, Lands and Parks.

Preston, Richard J. 2002. *Cree Narrative: Expressing the Personal Meanings of Events.* Montreal: McGill-Queen's University Press.

Pynn, Larry. 2000. *Last Stands: A Journey through North America's Vanishing Ancient Rainforests.* Corvallis: Oregon State University Press.

– 2006. 'Untamed Tatlatui.' *British Columbia Magazine* 48, no. 1:40–49.

Ridington, Robin. 1988. *Trail to Heaven: Knowledge and Narrative in a Northern Native Community.* Iowa City: University of Iowa Press.

– 1990a. 'Documenting the Normal, Perverting the Real: Contrasting Images of Native Indian Experience.' In *Trail to Heaven: Knowledge and Narrative in a Northern Native Community.* Iowa City: University of Iowa Press.

– 1990b. *Little Bit Know Something: Stories in a Language of Anthropology.* Iowa City: University of Iowa Press.

– 1990c. 'Technology, Worldview, and Adaptive Strategy in a Northern Hunting Society.' In *Little Bit Know Something: Stories in a Language of Anthropology.* Iowa City: University of Iowa Press.

Ridington, Robin, and Jillian Ridington. 2006. *When You Sing It Now, Just Like New: First Nations Poetics, Voices, and Representations.* Lincoln: University of Nebraska Press.

Rushforth, Scott, and James S. Chisholm. 1991. *Cultural Persistence: Continuity in Meaning and Moral Responsibility among the Bearlake Athapaskans.* Tucson: University of Arizona Press.

Sandlos, John. 2007. *Hunters at the Margin: Native People and Wildlife Conservation in the Northwest Territories.* Vancouver: UBC Press.

Saxon, Leslie. 1997. 'Tahltan Biological Words: Unpublished Word List, Collected at Iskut, B.C.' In possession of author, University of Victoria. Typescript; data input by Jillian Snider.

Schegloff, Emanuel A. 1997. '"Narrative Analysis" Thirty Years Later.' *Journal of Narrative and Life History* 7, no. 1–4:97–106.

Scott, Colin H., and Jeremy Webber. 2001. 'Conflicts between Cree Hunting and Sports Hunting: Co-Management Decision-Making at James Bay.' In *Aboriginal Autonomy and Development in Northern Quebec and Labrador,* ed. Colin H. Scott. Vancouver: UBC Press.

Shanklin, Eugenia. 1985. 'Sustenance and Symbol: Anthropological Studies of Domesticated Animals.' *Annual Review of Anthropology* 14:375–403.

Sharp, Henry S. 1976. 'Man:Wolf:Woman:Dog.' *Arctic Anthropology* 13, no. 1:25–34.

– 1986. 'Shared Experience and Magical Death: Chipewyan Explanations of a Prophet's Decline.' *Ethnology* 24, no. 4:257–70.

– 1994. 'Inverted Sacrifice.' In *Circumpolar Religion and Ecology: An Anthropology of the North,* ed. Takashi Irimoto and Takako Yamada. Tokyo: University of Tokyo Press.

– 2001. *Loon: Memory, Meaning, and Reality in a Northern Dene Community.* Lincoln: University of Nebraska Press.

Sheppard, Janice R. 1983a. 'The Dog Husband: Structural Identity and Emotional Specificity in Northern Athapaskan Oral Narrative.' *Arctic Anthropology* 20, no. 1:89–101.

– 1983b. 'The History and Values of a Northern Athapaskan Indian Village.' PhD diss., University of Wisconsin.

Smith, Anthony D. 1981. *The Ethnic Revival in the Modern World.* Cambridge: Cambridge University Press.

– 1986. *The Ethnic Origin of Nations.* New York: Basil Blackwell.

Smith, David M. 2002. 'The Flesh and the Word: Stories and Other Gifts of the Animals in Chipewyan Cosmology.' *Anthropology and Humanism* 27, no. 1:60–79.

Speck, Frank G. 1945. *The Celestial Bear Comes Down to Earth: The Bear Sacrifice Ceremony of the Munsee-Mahican in Canada as Related by Nekatcit.* Reading, PA: Science Press Printing Company.

Steward, Julian. 1960. 'Carrier Acculturation: The Direct Historical
    Approach.' In *Culture in History: Essays in Honor of Paul Radin,* ed. Stanley
    Diamond. New York: Columbia University Press.
Stone, Andrew J. 1896–97. Diaries and Journal of Andrew Jackson Stone.
    Bancroft Library, Berkeley, CA.
Tahltan Joint Councils. 1999. 'Tahltan Joint Councils Traditional Use Study:
    Documenting a Unique Cultural Landscape: Final Report.' Vol. 1. *Tatl'ah*
    and Victoria: Unpublished report prepared for the BC Ministry of Forests.
Tanner, Adrian. 1979. *Bringing Home Animals: Religious Ideology and Mode of
    Production of the Mistassani Cree Hunters.* London: C. Hurst and Company.
Teit, James A. 1906. 'Notes on the Tahltan Indians of British Columbia.' In
    *Boas Anniversary Volume: Anthropological Papers Written in Honor of Franz
    Boas on the Twenty-fifth Anniversary of His Doctorate,* ed. Berthold Laufer.
    New York: G.E. Stechert and Co.
– 1909. 'Two Tahltan Traditions.' *Journal of American Folklore* 22, no. 85:314–18.
– 1912–15a. Fieldnotes on the Tahltan Indians. Canadian Museum of
    Civilization, Gatineau, QC. Manuscript.
– 1912–15b. Report on Tahltan Fieldwork among the Tahltan, Kaska, and Bear
    Lake Indians. Canadian Museum of Civilization, Gatineau, QC, box 121,
    folder 3, 1210.4b, VI-O-8M. Typescript.
– 1917. 'Kaska Tales.' *Journal of American Folklore* 30, no. 118:427–73.
– 1919. 'Tahltan Tales.' *Journal of American Folklore* 32, no. 124:198–250.
– 1921a. 'Tahltan Tales.' *Journal of American Folklore* 34, no. 133:223–53.
– 1921b. 'Tahltan Tales.' *Journal of American Folklore* 34, no. 134:335–56.
– 1956. 'Field Notes on the Tahltan and Kaska Indians, 1912–15.'
    Anthropologica 3, no. 1:40–171.
Tennant, Paul. 1990. *Aboriginal Peoples and Politics: The Indian Land Question in
    British Columbia, 1849–1989.* Vancouver: UBC Press.
Thompson, Judy. 2007. *Recording Their Story: James Teit and the Tahltan.*
    Vancouver: Douglas and McIntyre.
Thornton, Thomas F. 2008. *Being and Place among the Tlingit.* Seattle: University
    of Washington Press.
Tobey, Margaret L. 1981. 'Carrier.' In *Handbook of North American Indians, Vol. 6:
    Subarctic,* ed. June Helm. Washington, DC: Smithsonian Institution Press.
Tsilhqot'in Nation v. British Columbia. 2007. Reasons for Judgment. Decision of
    the Supreme Court of British Columbia ([2007] BCSC 1700).
Turner, Nancy. 1997. 'Tahltan Traditional Plants.' Unpublished collection of
    plant names in English and Tahltan (with images).
Turner, Nancy J. 1998. *Plant Technology of First Peoples in British Columbia.*
    Vancouver: UBC Press.

Valentine, Lisa P. 1995. *Making It Their Own: Severn Ojibwe Communicative Practices*. Toronto: University of Toronto Press.

Vanstone, James W. 1974. *Athapaskan Adaptations: Hunters and Fishermen of the Subarctic Forests*. Chicago: Aldine Publishing Co.

Vayda, Andrew P., and Roy A. Rappaport. 1968. 'Ecology, Cultural and Noncultural.' In *Introduction to Cultural Anthropology*, ed. James A. Clifton. Boston: Houghton Mifflin Co.

Walker, T.A.T. 1976. *Spatsizi*. Smithers, BC: Harbour Publishing.

– Various dates. Walker Family and Business Papers (MS-2784). BC Archives and Records Service, Victoria.

Westman, Clinton M. 2010. 'Distorting the Aboriginal Industry: Widdowson, Howard, and Their Disputants.' *Anthropologica* 52, no. 1:201–6.

Widdowson, Frances, and Albert Howard. 2008. *Disrobing the Aboriginal Industry: The Deception Behind Indigenous Cultural Preservation*. Montreal: McGill-Queen's University Press.

Willerslev, Rane. 2007. *Soul Hunters: Hunting, Animism, and Personhood among the Siberian Yukaghirs*. Berkeley and Los Angeles: University of California Press.

Wolf, Eric R. 1972. 'Ownership and Political Ecology.' *Anthropological Quarterly* 45, no. 3:201–5.

Wooding, Frederick H. 1997. *Lake, River and Sea-Run Fishes of Canada*. Madeira Park, BC: Harbour Publishing.

Index

accordion model of communities in flux, 148n2

acculturation, 7, 127, 141n2

animals, 40; and caribou, 40, 70, 73–4; crow, 139n25; domesticates, 79–80; grizzly bear, 76; moose, 40, 69–70; raven, 139n25; sentience, 70, 123

anthropologists, 70, 123; and research by vehicle, 14, 31, 140n29

Asch, Michael, 28, 127

Basso, Keith H., 141n4

Bear Lake (place), 34–5, 44, 140n1

blockades, 29, 51, 119, 144n22; and at *Tl'abāne* (Klappan; 2005–2007), 126–30; at *Tlēgōhīn* (2005), 125

British Columbia Railway (rail grade), 29, 40, 49, 55–6, 78

bullshitting, 58

Campbell, Robert, 50

camping, 55–6, 140n30

cards (playing), 69, 75, 104

Caribou Hide, 35, 43–6

civil disobedience, 51. *See also* blockades

clans, 42–3; and symbols of, 107, 112

Clayoquot Sound, 127

Collingwood family, 102, 111

Commonage at *Tlēgōhīn*, 46–8, 99, 143n19

Cree (people), 127, 139n22, 140n28, 147nn10–12

Cruikshank, Julie, 19–20

culture: and authenticity, 115. *See also* hunting, as a cultural system

Dakelh (people), 141n2

Davis, Wade, 103, 142n5

Dease Lake. See *Tatl'ah*

Dease Lake Post, 49–50

Delgamuukw v. The Queen (1991), 14–15; 115

Delgamuukw v. The Queen (1997), 14–15, 149n9

Dene (people): and MacKenzie Valley Pipeline, 126–7

Deneka'ladiyah (story), 82, 118–20

Diaz, Robert N., 108

dogs, 42, 81–3; and ambivalence towards, 83, 147n8; Tahltan Bear Dog, 81, 146n3

ANTHROPOLOGICAL HORIZONS

Editor: Michael Lambek, University of Toronto

Published to date: